MAKE
THEIR
DAY!

MAKE THEIR DAY!

EMPLOYEE RECOGNITION THAT WORKS

PROVEN WAYS TO BOOST MORALE, PRODUCTIVITY, AND PROFITS

SECOND EDITION, REVISED AND EXPANDED

CINDY VENTRICE

BK

Berrett–Koehler Publishers, Inc.
San Francisco
a BK Business book

Berrett-Koehler Publishers, Inc.
235 Montgomery Street, Suite 650
San Francisco, CA 94104-2916
Tel: (415) 288-0260
Fax: (415) 362-2512
www.bkconnection.com

Ordering Information
Quantity sales. Special discounts are available on quantity purchases by corporations, associations, and others. For details, contact the "Special Sales Department" at the Berrett-Koehler address above.
Individual sales. Berrett-Koehler publications are available through most bookstores. They can also be ordered directly from Berrett-Koehler: Tel: (800) 929-2929; Fax: (802) 864-7626; www.bkconnection.com
Orders for college textbook/course adoption use. Please contact Berrett-Koehler: Tel: (800) 929-2929; Fax: (802) 864-7626.
Orders by U.S. trade bookstores and wholesalers. Please contact Ingram Publisher Ser-vices, Tel: (800) 509-4887; Fax: (800) 838-1149; E-mail: customer.service@ingrampublisherservices.com; or visit www.ingrampublisherservices.com/Ordering for details about electronic ordering.

Berrett-Koehler and the BK logo are registered trademarks of Berrett-Koehler Publishers, Inc.

Printed in the United States of America

Berrett-Koehler books are printed on long-lasting acid-free paper. When it is available, we choose paper that has been manufactured by environmentally responsible processes. These may include using trees grown in sustainable forests, incorporating recycled paper, minimizing chlorine in bleaching, or recycling the energy produced at the paper mill.

Production Management: Michael Bass Associates

Library of Congress Cataloging-in-Publication Data

Ventrice, Cindy, 1956-
   Make their day! : employee recognition that works / Cindy Ventrice. — 2nd ed.
      p. cm.
   Includes bibliographical references and index.
      ISBN 978-1-57675-601-0 (pbk. : alk. paper)
      1. Incentive awards—United States. 2. Employee motivation—United States. I. Title.
   HF5549.5.I5V336 2009
   658.3'142—dc22   2009003710

Second Edition
14 13 12 11 10 09   10 9 8 7 6 5 4 3 2 1

To those who are striving
to create a better workplace.

contents

PART TWO
Whose Job Is Recognition, Anyway?

PART THREE
Making Recognition Work

foreword

For the past quarter century, I've had one of the truly great jobs in journalism. My beat has been the workplace—specifically, great workplaces. It's been my lucky lot to visit and write about companies that employees rave about in a variety of books and magazine articles. For the past half-dozen years, I've worked with my fellow journalist Milton Moskowitz to identify and write about the "100 Best Companies to Work For in America" for *Fortune*.

These companies represent the spectrum of the business world and have ranged from extremely familiar names like Google and Cisco to relative unknowns like Plante & Moran and Griffin Hospital. Regardless of the industry, size, age, or location of the companies, I've noticed that employees of these terrific workplaces invariably talk about how they feel treated as individuals, that they feel respected, that they feel the management recognizes their contributions to the organization.

As I've looked more closely at these companies, I've learned that it is no accident that employees feel so positively about their employers. Great workplaces are the result of the attitudes and actions of management. At the core, the management of these companies sincerely believes that the employees are the ones who are primarily responsible for the success (or failure) of the enterprise. As a result of this attitude, management sees the need to constantly recognize the value of the employees. They see positive recognition as part of their jobs, not as something that occurs once every five years when it is time to hand out the employee recognition awards.

Even in a bad workplace, it would not be surprising to find an individual manager who is good about showing appreciation toward employees. But how can this happen throughout an organization? This is precisely what *Make Their Day!* is all about—how to make employee recognition part of the fabric of an organization.

It is a great pleasure to recommend this newly revised and expanded version of *Make Their Day!* as this is no ordinary management book. Cindy Ventrice has done her homework. She has looked at a variety of companies and interviewed dozens of managers to look beneath the surface. There are many books on employee recognition, but this one is by far the best. Most books on this subject give examples of best practices in the field—in some cases hundreds of such examples. The idea seems to be that to improve employee recognition, managers should copy the policy or practice used by another organization.

The problem is that each company is unique. Each one has its own distinctive culture and history. What works in one company may completely backfire in another. But the approach of many managers simply ignores this seemingly obvious fact. Imitate what Company A does and you, too, will be successful.

That's where *Make Their Day!* can be so useful. Ventrice's book is full of lots of useful and provocative examples. But she goes beyond merely reciting cases. Using her in-depth interviews with managers at a variety of companies, Ventrice explores the deeper issues involved. Many of the companies she cites have made our *Fortune* list, and I can testify that she has captured what's special about how these companies recognize employees. She puts her finger on the all-important question of trust. How can you recognize people in such a way that trust is built? She points out that it is a question of relationships, not techniques. She shows that genuinely recognizing people means doing it all the time, not just on special occasions.

This book offers precisely the kind of insights that any manager interested in creating a great workplace should read.

ROBERT LEVERING

———————————

Robert Levering is coauthor of *Fortune*'s annual "100 Best Companies to Work For in America" and cofounder of Great Place to Work® Institute.

I am excited to be bringing you this completely updated second edition of *Make Their Day!* Because companies are continually changing and evolving, I have updated the stories of the companies featured in the original edition. In some cases, I have retained examples of programs that companies are no longer using because the examples make an important point. With others there have been new developments that I believe will interest you. You will find that there are new examples from organizations such as Best Buy, Cisco, and Google demonstrating important recognition concepts. There are also new stories, insights, tips, and tools throughout that will help you provide the best possible recognition to your team!

I have added two chapters to this edition. The first addresses organizational culture. This chapter will help you, the manager, determine the effect that age, nationality, proximity to you, and even job description have on recognition preferences. The second new chapter addresses fairness. In my work, I have found that fairness is an ever-increasing manager concern that seems in direct conflict with the ability to individualize and personalize recognition. This chapter will help you provide recognition that is both fair and meaningful.

Most important, this edition zeroes in on what you—the manager, supervisor, or team leader—can do to create an environment where people feel valued. You will be introduced to the concepts of *Make Their Day* recognition and shown how you can apply them to your work situation.

While focused on the manager, this book is loaded with information that anyone can use. Human resource groups will get ideas on how they can administer more effective programs. Individuals in any role will learn how to recognize their coworkers, their managers and supervisors, and even themselves. Most of the concepts are just as applicable outside work. According to my college intern, "This stuff even works on my roommates!"

A lot has changed in this edition. One thing that hasn't changed is the amount of money wasted on recognition that doesn't work. In the first edition, I estimated that every year U.S. companies spend about $18 billion on recognition and incentives.[1] That number is probably quite conservative. The International Society for Performance Improvement believes it to be closer to $27 billion for noncash incentives alone![2] Eighty-nine percent of organizations have some kind of recognition program in place,[3] yet most employees still feel inadequately recognized. According to Gallup research, 65 percent of employees reported receiving no recognition in the previous year.[4]

How is it that we can spend so much and achieve so little? This is the question that led to *Make Their Day!* I wanted to know what would really boost employee recognition satisfaction. My initial research included interviews with hundreds of employees. I asked them to describe examples of meaningful recognition. Since the initial publication, I have conducted additional research. I have been able to better quantify what employees want. I have gathered information as it relates to generation, location, and years in the workforce. You will find this research, along with lots of new examples from readers and clients. I hope you find this new expanded edition to be a valuable tool for creating an energizing work environment.

CINDY VENTRICE
SANTA CRUZ, CALIFORNIA,
MARCH 2009

Real Results

A new sales manager is given the second-lowest-performing region. He believes that people who feel valued will outperform others and so he decides to make recognition a priority. His first quarter as manager, his team beats its quota. The second quarter they do it again, and at the end of the third quarter . . . well, at the end of the third quarter they are the second-highest-performing region!

They went from second-lowest-performing
to second-highest in nine months.

It is a simple fact: people who feel valued perform at a much higher level. Think about a great manager you've had, one who made you feel valued. What would you have done to make him or her look good? I know the answer. A lot!

An executive leaves one company for another. With him, he takes his "good, solid performers." The new company is built on a culture of recognition. Once he adapts to their style, he says, "My good, solid performers became stars."

His good, solid performers became stars.

Wouldn't you like to have a few more stars on your team? With a little time and effort to offer meaningful recognition, you will see significant results.

Results that you can see—that is what this book is about. *Make Their Day!* will introduce you to *recognition that works—* recognition that is meaningful, memorable, and boosts morale, productivity, and profits. As you read this book, you will learn simple, effective techniques that you can begin to implement today.

Making Recognition a Priority

I know you're busy. You have to make sure the work gets done. You may even be dealing with hiring freezes, layoffs, mergers and acquisitions, strikes, budget cuts, rising expenses, product defects, missed deadlines, or high turnover among in-demand workers. There's a good chance that, in addition to your managerial duties, you are also an individual contributor. In terms of priorities, if you're like many managers, supervisors, and team leaders, recognition has come dead last. While this may be understandable, it is a big mistake. Managing is easier, not harder, when you make recognition a priority.

Don't Put Recognition on Your To-Do List

After reading the heading for this section, you're probably thinking, "What do you mean, don't put recognition on your to-do list? If it's not on my to-do list, how can recognition be a priority? Isn't that a contradiction?" No, it isn't. I've seen many managers and supervisors who decided to make recognition a priority. They had the best intentions when they put "recognize employees" on to their to-do lists, and then, as the weeks progressed and pressing matters demanded their attention, they slowly moved recognition farther and farther down the list. Even though their intentions were good, recognition never happened.

You have enough to do already! If you add recognition to your oversized to-do list, there is a good chance that you won't get to it. When you do manage to get to it, you're likely to do it once, check it off, and then forget about it. This isn't the kind of recognition that works.

Make Recognition the Header on Your To-Do List

Recognition isn't something you can do and then check off your list. You need to think of recognition a little differently. Instead of adding recognition to your to-do list, make it *the header*. Find ways to make recognition part of every employee interaction. When you delegate, add a little praise of past accomplishments. When you receive project updates, thank employees for their promptness, thoroughness, or accuracy. When you hold a team meeting to talk about a new challenge, express confidence in the group's ability to meet that challenge. As you complete each item on your to-do list, think about how you can incorporate recognition into it.

Make Your Job Easier!

Make recognition the header on your list, and you will find your job gets easier. There are hundreds of small things you can do to provide the recognition your employees crave without putting a greater strain on your time, things that positively affect the work environment because they provide the right kind of recognition. With the right recognition, you will find employees more willing to tackle problems on their own instead of bringing them to you to solve. With the right recognition, employees will show more concern about quality and reputation. With the right recognition, employees will be more willing to pitch in when things get difficult. Morale will go up. Absenteeism will go down. And your job will get easier.

Recognition that works does this: it energizes and revitalizes the workplace. It creates a loyal, motivated, and productive workforce. And a loyal, motivated, and productive workforce makes your job as a manager easier.

Recognition That Works, *Works*!

Recognition that works, *works*—even in the most challenging situations. Nothing demonstrates this quite as well as the story of Remedy Support Services that was featured in the first edition of this book.

> In August 2001, Peregrine Systems purchased competitor Remedy Corporation. While managers at Remedy were hopeful that the purchase would help them expand their operations and increase market share, they still faced typical merger issues: concerns about possible layoffs, culture changes, product direction, and the priorities of the parent company—challenges that many managers are very familiar with. During the next eight months, Peregrine Systems endured the same financial setbacks as most of the technology industry and suffered through the seemingly inevitable layoffs.

This was only the beginning of the challenges that Remedy faced as part of Peregrine Systems. Peregrine announced it had misstated revenue during the past two years, and the CEO and CFO resigned.[1] Remedy was restructured, and 5 percent of the workforce was laid off. Peregrine stock continued a steady decline; class action stockholder lawsuits accumulated; and by the time Remedy had been part of Peregrine Systems for ten months, Peregrine stock had been delisted from NASDAQ.[2] Just over twelve months after it was acquired by Peregrine Systems, Remedy was sold to BMC Software.

Talk about a whirlwind of turmoil and change! Given the circumstances, it's easy to imagine employee morale would be at an all-time low. How could managers possibly keep employees productive under these conditions? Yet during the tumultuous ten-month period from purchase to delisting, Remedy Support Service maintained employee morale and improved customer satisfaction ratings while continuing to grow its revenue stream![3]

Mike Little, then VP of Worldwide Professional Services and Support, said the company survived and even thrived because the managerial staff set big goals, listened to employees, and showed their appreciation. As you will discover as you read this book, these three things are keys to offering meaningful and memorable recognition.

Visible Signs of Recognition

To bring employees through this crisis, Remedy Support Services used many forms of recognition. Pirate ships constructed by each of Remedy's support groups offered a reminder of a friendly competition to be the best support team. Some managers gave out stickers for perfect customer surveys, and employees displayed the stickers outside their cubicles. One employee was proud of a toy SUV his manager had presented him in recognition of his good work. Managers worked hard to find fun and creative ways to improve performance and show employees they were valued.

Managers also held Employee Appreciation Days where they washed employees' cars, prepared them food, played games, and dressed up in costumes. According to employees, Employee Appreciation Days isn't an event the organization simply puts on; it's something the managers do for them. When I met with employees, they were getting ready to celebrate Employee Appreciation Days. Because of budget cutbacks, little discretionary money was available. Many employees told me that instead of eliminating the celebration, managers chose to pay for it out of their own pockets. The gesture wasn't lost on the employees. It meant a lot to them.

Invisible Recognition

Many companies try friendly competitions, prizes, and events with little or no success. These things only worked for Remedy because managers offered another kind of recognition as well— recognition that you might not even notice at first glance.

When I toured Remedy with Mike Little, he introduced me to many of the hundred-plus employees in support services. During those introductions, I discovered he knew everyone's name, how long each had been with the company, and where they had worked before. There was an easy camaraderie between Little and the unit's employees. It was apparent that one way he recognized employee value was by staying in touch with and caring about every individual.

Here is another example of this more subtle form of recognition. One of Remedy's tenets is "Hire the best and then trust them." There is a lot of recognition in that statement *if managers really believe it*. Remedy managers proved they meant it when Peregrine Systems required a

second round of layoffs. These managers refused to follow outlined procedures. During the first round, they had
followed protocol: personnel followed laid-off employees
to their desks, waited while they packed up their belong-
ings, and then escorted them out of the building. Following this first round of layoffs, managers asked themselves,
"Where is the trust in doing it this way?" They hated the
message their actions sent.

During the second round, they handled it differently.
They allowed employees to spend as much time as they
liked packing up their things and saying their good-byes.
No one followed them around, and no one restricted their
access. Some employees finished quickly, and others spent
the entire day. Several thanked their managers for allowing them to leave in this manner. The way the managers
handled the layoff was a small gesture, but it meant a lot
to employees—both those who stayed and those who left.

Managers at Remedy built recognition into every action and
reaction. It was the header on their to-do list, and it made all the
difference to employees. It is the reason why, in the face of
unbelievable turmoil, Remedy Support Services consistently
improved customer satisfaction and increased revenue. As you
read the chapters that follow, you will learn why the people in
your workplace consider the kinds of recognition that Remedy
offered to be so important.

Proven Techniques

Throughout this book, you will learn about organizations that have
demonstrated their ability to offer effective recognition. These
organizations, as a whole, experience lower turnover and higher
productivity and profitability than their industry averages. This
point bears repeating: When employees give high ratings to the

recognition they receive, their organizations typically have lower turnover and higher productivity and profitability than other organizations in the same industry! During economic downturns, these organizations lay off fewer employees; and, when they do have to reduce their workforce, employee morale is far more resilient.

The firms that make *Fortune* magazine's annual list of the "100 Best Companies to Work For" provide great examples of organizations that offer many forms of effective recognition. According to Robert Levering, who along with Milton Moskowitz oversees *Fortune*'s Best Companies project, "No company can have a great place to work without having good ways to show appreciation to employees." Not only do the companies on the list do a good job of offering the kind of recognition employees value, but these companies also receive tremendous payback for their efforts. Levering and Moskowitz's research reveals the following:

- Industry by industry, the companies on the list have 50 percent less turnover than their counterparts.
- Publicly traded companies on the list average a 15 to 25 percent greater return for investors than the S&P 500 over three-, five-, and ten-year periods.

The *Make Their Day!* philosophy is based on proven techniques. Each organization, department, manager, or supervisor highlighted in this book will help you understand what it takes to create meaningful recognition.

In the chapters that follow, you will learn how to create meaningful and memorable recognition that improves employee commitment to your organization. You will learn how to offer recognition that works and begin to look at recognition differently. You will train yourself to see what the recipient sees, looking past superficial symbols and focusing on what really matters. In the process, you will reduce your workload, improve productivity, and create a workplace where people love to work.

PART 1

Employees Want to Love Their Work

chapter **1**

Recognition That Works

"Please, not another T-shirt!"

"I resent the money that's spent to purchase doodads. It could be spent much more wisely."

"Certificates of appreciation? I hate the damn things."

I assume this isn't the reaction you expect from recognition. Yet, if you depend on your organization to fulfill your employees' need for recognition, there is a good chance that your employees would express similar opinions.

According to a former employee of one technology company:

> "Our company offered the Terrific Employee Award. Everyone thought it was a cheesy name. People didn't know why they were being awarded. It became a joke. The CEO never got involved. No one but HR took it seriously. They solicited employees for nominations and got so few responses they eventually gave up and selected someone themselves. The awards were gift certificates. They were nice, but without meaning."

Missing the Mark

When you think of recognition, what comes to mind? Do you think of raises, bonuses, stock awards, gift certificates, parties, prizes, and plaques? Many managers view these things as recognition, but they are wrong. Employees see it differently.

According to employees, 57 percent of the
most meaningful recognition is free!

That's right: in an international survey in 2007, I found that 57 percent of the most meaningful recognition doesn't even cost a dollar!

Like the person in the last example, employees are looking for meaning, *not things*. They see tangible awards as a vehicle for *delivering* recognition, but they don't regard the awards themselves *as* recognition. They're much more interested in the underlying message behind the reward.

Your employees are strong believers in the old saying "It's the thought that counts." For awards to count as recognition, your employees need to see acknowledgment of their specific accomplishments and sincere appreciation of their personal value to the organization. The following examples will illustrate why recognition often misses the mark.

Perks Aren't Recognition

The director of a small nonprofit agency hosts a dinner on a Friday night for employees and volunteers. Everyone has a great time and goes back to work the following Monday feeling refreshed and energized. The director planned this event as a form of recognition. Although it was fun and boosted morale, it wasn't recognition; it was a perk—a little something extra.

To add an element of recognition, the director can announce that the dinner is a way of thanking the group for something they have accomplished; for example, "We served ten thousand clients this year, and we couldn't have done it without your help." She can include an after-dinner presentation during which she tells detailed stories about the specific ways in which employees and volunteers helped accomplish this feat. Her message will provide the recognition.

Bonuses Aren't Recognition

The owner of an insurance agency gives holiday bonuses. They come in handy when employees head out to do their last-minute shopping. Employees appreciate the bonus but don't see it as recognition. They expect it and feel entitled to it. Many have already budgeted for it, and if it is less than they anticipated, employees are resentful. If the bonus is more than was expected, they're pleasantly surprised but figure they must have earned it.

The owner of the agency thinks the bonuses are a form of recognition, but employees don't agree. To provide recognition, the owner needs to tie the bonuses to an achievement. But that isn't enough. He also needs to state that the bonuses are his way of showing appreciation: "Our customer service ratings are up 10 percent over last year. That increase has helped us better position ourselves in the market. I know we couldn't have done it without all of your hard work, and I want to show my appreciation by giving each of you this bonus." Without the tie-in and the statement of appreciation, the bonus is just another way in which employees get paid.

Plaques and Awards Aren't Recognition

Each month in a staff meeting, the manager of a city public works department presents one employee with a plaque and a gift certificate. As she hands out the awards, she explains that the recipient is "doing a good job" and is a "great employee." She believes she is recognizing employees, but employees in her department have no idea what it takes to get the award. This public award is supposed to be recognition, but these employees see it as favoritism and feel even less recognized. If employees, including the recipients, don't understand why recognition is given, then recognition hasn't taken place.

If this manager establishes criteria for the award such as excellence in customer service or cost cutting, and then describes what the recipient did to earn the award, then the award will provide recognition.

Incentives Aren't Recognition

A manufacturer sets up a quota system for assemblers: when they reach a certain level, they will receive a $100 gift certificate. As assemblers reach their quota, they find their certificate tucked in their pay envelope. Their supervisor thinks the certificates are recognition, but they aren't. They are incentives. They tell employees, "If you do this, you will get that." Used properly, incentives can motivate people to do more, but there really isn't much recognition built in.

The line supervisor can easily add an element of recognition to the incentive. If he hand-delivers the certificate, personally congratulates the recipient, and offers appreciation for a job well done, then the incentive will have recognition value.

There's a lot you can do that will make people feel recognized, but first you have to be clear about what recognition *isn't*. It isn't perks, bonuses, plaques and awards, or incentives. While these things aren't recognition, they can be a highly valued part of the recognition experience. They can serve as excellent concrete reminders of the recognition you offer.

An employee who does customer support offers the following example:

> "I was given a tough customer to assist. The underlying message was 'We don't entrust really important relationships to just anybody. We believe in you. You have proven yourself.' After I was successful, they let me pick from a catalog of gifts. The opportunity was the recognition, but the mixer I selected reminds me of it—every time I walk into the kitchen."

Don't make the mistake of thinking that the awards are the recognition. If you do, you will fall into a common trap: assuming that all you need to make recognition work is a new award. Focus only on the tangible award, and recognition will most likely fail. Focus on the *meaning* behind the award, and employees will receive recognition that works.

This isn't to say that looking for new award ideas doesn't have value. It's always a good idea to come up with new and creative ways to show recognition. Many excellent books are filled with great recognition ideas. Two that I would recommend are *1001 Ways to Reward Employees* by Bob Nelson and *301 Ways to Have Fun at Work* by Dave Hemsath and Leslie Yerkes. Nothing is wrong with getting ideas. In fact, the *Make Their Day* website offers a free weekly tip subscription that will provide you with lots of new ideas. By all means, get creative.

Remember, *57 percent of surveyed employees said the most meaningful recognition was free!* Eighty-eight percent said it cost under $100. What makes recognition meaningful isn't the award; it is the meaning behind the award.

> **Before you give an award ask yourself a few questions:**
>
> - What achievement does the award recognize?
> - How are the recipients selected?
> - When and how are awards presented?
> - What can I do to make sure that the award provides recognition?

What Makes Recognition Work

Simple, thoughtful gestures are what employees tell me make their day. Here are some examples:

☑ A souvenir from your vacation
☑ Remembering the details of an employee's project
☑ A thank-you e-mail
☑ A handwritten note

The hundreds of stories that I've heard confirm that recognition doesn't have to be big and splashy to be memorable and meaningful. What stands out in employees' minds is recognition that is memorable because of the consistency and regularity with which it is offered, sometimes because it is clever and unique, but most often because it sends a strong message that they are valued.

> rec·og·ni·tion (rĕkə'g-nĭsh'ən) *n.* **1. the act of seeing or identifying. 2. the perception of something as existing or true. 3. the acknowledgment of something as valid or entitled to consideration.**

Look up *recognize* and *recognition* in any dictionary, and you will find definitions that use words like *see*, *identify*, and *acknowledge*. These words are at the core of how employees define recognition. One man told me, "I'd be happy if I thought anyone here even knew I existed." Most employees don't feel anywhere near this level of dissatisfaction, but his comment does show the extreme of what it means to feel completely unrecognized.

Another told me about how much more productive she was when she had the cubicle outside her manager's office. She emphasized that she wasn't intimidated, just visible.

Employees want to be seen—sometimes literally. When anyone higher up the organizational ladder greets an employee by name in the hallway, typically that employee will view the greeting as a form of recognition. Why? Because these are the people who employees most want to be seen by because they have the most influence over their careers.

Employees also want their accomplishments identified and acknowledged. When coworkers, internal customers, managers,

---

How well do you see employees? Here is a visibility quiz for you:

Imagine a senior manager stops by during your team meeting. Could you, if asked, introduce each individual in the room by providing the following information?

- ☐ Name
- ☐ Length of time with the company
- ☐ Role on the team
- ☐ Special strengths
- ☐ Current project and why it is important

If you don't have all of this information right on the tip of your tongue, work on it. Great leaders really know the people on their teams.

and supervisors provide specific details about the value of an employee's contribution, they provide recognition that works at its most fundamental level.

The Elements of Recognition

Recognition that works has four basic elements: praise, thanks, opportunity, and respect. Every successful gesture of recognition includes at least one of these four basic elements and is typically a combination of more than one. If you don't include at least one of the elements, you aren't giving recognition. You're giving an incentive, prize, gift, or plaque, but not recognition that works. Let's look at each element separately.

Praise

Employees want to hear you say, "Hey, you accomplished something important." They want you to acknowledge their progress. They want you to notice what they do right.

Here are three tips for offering praise:

- Be clear and concise about what you are praising.
- Make the praise proportional to the accomplishment. Don't exaggerate or overdo it.
- Keep it timely. Don't wait six months for the performance review. When you see it or hear about it, praise it.

You can praise employees publicly or privately. Be aware that while every employee wants praise, not all employees want public praise. It's up to you to learn each employee's preference. For more on this topic, see Chapter 12.

Thanks

A sincere thank-you is a highly valued form of recognition that works. Some managers think there is no need to thank a person who is doing his or her job. It's true that you don't *have* to thank each employee, but if someone's efforts make your job easier, then thank that person. Everyone responds to heartfelt appreciation. Employees will work many times harder for managers who express their gratitude. Offer a sincere thank-you, and you will make significant progress in improving morale and productivity.

To make sure that your thank-you has the desired effect, describe why the person is being thanked. Be specific, accurate, clear, and concise.

Remember: the simplest and frequently most desired form of recognition is a simple expression of gratitude.

Put It in Writing

While you're at it, think about providing your praise and appreciation in the form of a handwritten note. People tell me they hang on to these for years and pull them out when they need a boost. Talk about a great return on the time you have to invest in writing the note!

Opportunity

At first glance, opportunity doesn't appear to be an element of recognition, but it's actually a very important element of recognition that works. Over half of the examples of meaningful recognition that I have heard include this element. Give your employees new opportunities to contribute in a meaningful way and learn new skills, provide them with more freedom in how the work gets done, and they will be committed to you and your department's success.

Consider these opportunity tips:

- Learn about employees' workplace aspirations.
- Assess their ability and desire to work effectively with little supervision.
- Coach them on what they need to do to achieve their goals.
- Offer learning opportunities that will help them reach those goals.
- Increase their freedom in incremental stages as they demonstrate their ability to work well on their own.

The results will be happy, productive employees who never want to leave!

Respect

Respect is an often overlooked element of recognition. In reality, it is the most crucial element. You've heard the phrase "You must be present to win." Well, respect must be present for recognition to take place.

Consider employee needs as you make decisions, and you recognize employee value. Stop and listen, make allowances for personal crises, get to know something about each person who works with you, and you show respect.

Focusing on respect along with praise, thanks, and opportunity means that you'll be offering meaningful, memorable recognition that boosts morale and productivity.

TAKING ACTION

Here are a few things you can do to ensure that you offer recognition that works:

- Make sure employees feel like you are seeing and acknowledging them. Look for ways to simplify. You don't have to be clever—just sincere.
- Assess all tangible awards for recognition potential. Just because the incentives, perks, and celebrations aren't in and of themselves recognition doesn't mean you can't add an element of recognition to make them more meaningful.
- Continue reading for more ways to make their day!

chapter 2

Finding Recognition Everywhere

I am making a difference.
My company invests in my development.
I receive challenging assignments.
I am proud of where I work.
My supervisor trusts me to do my best.

When employees make statements such as these, they are describing recognition that comes from the work and the workplace. They feel valued without being told they are valuable. This is inherent recognition.

Every day employees everywhere look for proof they are valued. Not only do they want their managers to tell them they are important, but they also want them to show it. They want to work for a manager who builds recognition into everyday occurrences. They want to work where recognition is inherent in the way they are treated and in the work they do. Let's look at how you can do that.

Plante & Moran

Company recruiters visit college campuses every year. They want to lure the best and the brightest to their organizations. They paint an appealing picture of what awaits these college graduates. Recruiters tell these potential hires that they will be a valuable part of their team if only they will choose to work for them. Once hired, these new employees often find the situation a little different from what the recruiters described. Only a small percentage of organizations demonstrate, in any meaningful way, that they really believe the positive things their recruiters say to lure new hires.

Plante & Moran, a Midwest-based midsized accounting firm, is an exception. Its new hires know from the moment they arrive that they're valued. On their first day of work, new recruits receive business cards, manuals that will help them do their jobs well, and their own office with their name outside the door. They're assigned two people: one a supervising partner, and the other an experienced coworker called a "buddy." These two people help them adapt to work life and excel in their new careers. Plante & Moran provides concrete recognition of the value of new employees from the moment they are hired.

Employees see recognition in small gestures like receiving a nameplate on their first day and in bigger gestures like having a partner assigned to help them thrive and excel. The Plante & Moran new-hire process addresses the need for both respect and opportunity, two of the four elements of recognition. Employees there know they are valued. They know they are part of an organization where management wants to help them succeed.

It takes planning, preparation, and follow-through to make recognition part of the environment itself. The new-hire orientation at Plante & Moran is one example of how an organization does this. As a manager, you can learn from Plante & Moran's success. Make a fuss over new hires:

☑ Send "welcome to our team" cards to their homes.

☑ Provide all the resources they need to get started.

☑ Take the team to lunch on new employees' first days.

☑ Assign "buddies" to orient them to the workplace.

☑ Connect often to see how you can assist them.

More examples in this chapter describe how you can create inherent recognition. First let's take a brief look at motivation theory and how it impacts your ability to recognize employees.

Understanding the Motivation Connection

Motivation can be intrinsic, extrinsic, or some combination of the two. Extrinsic motivation comes from outside the individual. Extrinsic motivators are the incentives that you can offer: the promise of a bonus if certain criteria are met, the prize in a contest, and the lure of a raise if a project is completed on time. Used properly, these types of incentives can work well,[1] but there isn't much recognition built into them.

Used improperly, incentives damage motivation. One seminar participant told me, "I have a supervisor who complains about employees in our unit and then gives them a cash award in hopes that they will improve. What she should be doing is working to get rid of them." This supervisor has damaged employee trust and is no longer respected. Employees in her department are *less* likely to feel motivated to perform.

In contrast to extrinsic motivation, intrinsic motivation comes from within. Individuals motivate themselves based on their own personal needs and expectations. Intrinsic motivation varies from person to person, with each individual being motivated by something slightly different from anyone else. A model of intrinsic motivation developed by David McClelland[2] says that what motivates us falls into three basic categories:

- **Achievement.** People motivated by achievement want to do something important or create something of value. They want to be valued for what they do.
- **Affiliation.** People motivated by affiliation want to belong. They want to be part of something bigger than themselves. They want to be valued for who they are and the company they keep.
- **Power/control.** People motivated by power and control want to have an impact on others or the environment. They want to be valued for how they change the world.

In varying degrees, these three motivators drive all of us.

A biotech scientist might find motivation in her desire to make a discovery that would have an impact on the health and well-being of cancer victims (achievement and power/control).

A line worker might care more about producing quality work (achievement) and belonging to a team (affiliation).

What effective recognition does best is acknowledge and support people's intrinsic motivators, and inherent recognition—recognition that comes from the work and workplace—often does this best. For instance, the biotech scientist in the example above would see additional funding for her research as a valuable form of recognition because it validates the importance of her work. Her manager's efforts to get project funding, whether successful or not, recognize her potential to achieve and her ability to make a difference. The primary purpose of securing funding is to go forward with the research, not to recognize the employee. Yet the employee will feel recognized. That is inherent recognition—recognition that is built right into the work and workplace.

For the line worker who is motivated by affiliation and achievement, the supervisor can have a positive impact by supporting the team in its efforts to improve performance. The line supervisor might champion his team's suggestion to change workflow in order to reduce the defect rate simply because he wants to see a reduction in the defect rate. Yet the employee motivated by affiliation and achievement will feel recognized because of the inherent recognition that comes from the supervisor's support.

What are the intrinsic motivators for the individuals on your team? How can you reinforce these motivators through the work and workplace?

- **Achievement.** Focus on results. Set individual goals and celebrate success. Provide new tasks that build on past achievements.
- **Affiliation.** Focus on the team. Set team goals and celebrate team success. Provide social opportunities and awards that demonstrate that they are part of the team.
- **Power/control.** Focus on positive effect. Are they improving the environment, making the streets safe, providing a phenomenal customer experience?

Recognizing Purpose and Quality

Purpose is a powerful motivator. The inherent recognition in having a common purpose comes from seeing progress toward goals that have a positive effect. Just ask the employees of most nonprofit agencies devoted to providing social services. If they know what their agency is trying to achieve and they believe they are making a contribution to those goals, they feel a strong sense of satisfaction. Many work willingly for much lower pay than they would in private industry because they believe they're making a difference.

Contrast the nonprofit example with the bureaucracy of some large organizations. You have probably heard more than a few jokes that make fun of bureaucracies. But it's no longer funny when you find yourself having to deal with a bureaucratic agency or giant conglomerate. Have you ever experienced a situation where you had a problem and couldn't get anyone to help you? Did employees recite policies that made no sense? Did they shuffle you from department to department until you became frustrated by their lack of concern and caring? Coping with a bureaucracy can quickly wear you down.

Imagine how unmotivated the employees in these organizations must feel. They have to work all day, every day, in an environment that frustrates and drains *you* in only a matter of moments. In this type of atmosphere, it is difficult to retain a sense of purpose. There is little motivation to do good work. They produce results of subpar quality. Employees are disconnected from the recognition that is inherent in doing valued work.

Employees want to take pride in their organization. They receive a form of recognition when they say, "I work for XYZ company," when XYZ company has a reputation for serving its community and producing quality products and services.

In the 2007 survey employees completed for *Fortune* magazine's "100 Best Companies to Work For" list, nearly all Google employees said they were proud to tell others where they work. Googlers, as they are called, are proud of their product. One hundred percent of employees use the Google search engine over the competition. They believe their product is the best and adds value to people's lives. They are also proud of the good works the company does, including green initiatives. According to one employee, "The 'don't be evil' mantra is more than skin deep; it is the core of the culture." Google provides a great example of the recognition that is inherent in purpose and quality.

Every job, unless it's illegal or immoral,
can have a mission or purpose that makes work
meaningful and creates inherent recognition.

Consider the employees who work the counter at the Department of Motor Vehicles (DMV). Many DMV offices act as purposeless bureaucracies with unengaged workers. Within that environment, a dynamic supervisor can still motivate employees by helping them recognize how they contribute to the public good. Suddenly those same workers aren't just shuffling papers. They are doing their part to make the streets safe for the public by testing drivers' knowledge, verifying that drivers are insured, and requiring proof that vehicles don't spew pollutants.

What if you're the broker of a real estate office? Do your agents and employees simply deal in property sales, or do they help people fulfill their dreams of owning a home? If you help them identify a purpose that creates a sense of pride, you have helped develop inherent recognition. Agents and employees with a higher purpose are far more likely to be enthusiastic and meticulous in their work. There is far more recognition in helping people fulfill their dreams than there is in selling houses.

Regardless of what your group does, it has a worthwhile purpose. Help your people find that purpose. Help them provide services or products of exceptional quality. Continually work to improve the group's reputation within the organization and your community. Remember that one of the elements of recognition is opportunity. Give employees the opportunity to contribute in a meaningful way. Acknowledge their progress. Doing so will create inherent recognition. When people are part of a team that knows that their work is making a difference, they receive recognition that works.

Recognizing Trustworthiness

People want to be trusted to do the right thing. Managers who demonstrate trust by providing unlimited access to information and giving employees the freedom to work flexible hours, telework, make decisions without someone's approval, or do the job as they see fit so long as they meet objectives are recognizing that employees have the best interests of the organization at heart and can be trusted to do what is right. Trusting employees provides two elements of recognition: respect and opportunity.

At Best Buy's corporate offices, managers have used this concept to completely revamp their culture. They consider theirs a results-only work environment (ROWE). Employees are free to come and go as they please. They choose how, where, and when the work gets done. The only measure is *whether* the work gets done. Since implementing this change, voluntary turnover has decreased and productivity is up 42 percent.

According to Amy Johnson, Demand Planning Manager, who worked for a manager who offered ROWE-type scheduling early on, "She treated us like grown-ups. . . . It made me feel so energized."

To manage effectively, the Best Buy managers I spoke with say you need to do all of the following:

- Have clear expectations.
- Ask your employees if they can commit to goals.
- Eliminate roadblocks to success.
- Trust and let go, but check in often for status reports.

Best Buy managers say that when you give people absolute freedom in how, where, and when the work gets done, some may test the boundaries for a couple of weeks, and then most will settle in. One or two under-performers will become obvious, and you will have to work with them to get them acclimated to working in this environment.

Ironically, they say that by focusing on results, it may feel like you are micromanaging. Frequent status meetings, until commonplace, can feel like you are checking up on people. You may also have people who aren't comfortable with determining how the work gets done. You will have to work with that.

Tyler Rebman, Director of Local Insights, who manages a ROWE team, says he once had a manager who said, "You are a big boy/girl. I trust you to do what is right." And according to Rebman, "That is the essence." The freedom and flexibility at Best Buy shows employees they are valued.

Recognizing Individual Value

Opportunities for Growth

Employees want to be recognized for their achievements, but they also want to know they are valued as people—that they are respected for who they are, not just what they do. One way you show employees they are valued is by providing opportunities for growth.

> The people at Plante & Moran know they are valued, in part, because the organization does such an exceptional job of helping people learn, develop, and grow. Managers focus on retaining people by meeting their need for new opportunities and challenges. They recognize people's value by ensuring that they are doing a job that provides satisfaction. To do this, employees are encouraged to use Plante & Moran's in-house vocational counselors. If someone is bored with auditing, the vocational counselors will help that employee find a new challenge appropriate to his or her skills, aptitude, and interests. Usually employees are able to stay within the company,

perhaps moving to a position where they offer investment advice, expert testimony, or handle mergers and acquisitions. Occasionally, employees discover a passion that just can't be filled within an accounting firm. Plante & Moran's vocational counselors still assist these employees in the process and have, on occasion, counseled employees who go on to become doctors, priests, and even, in one case, a disc jockey. They lose a few people, but at the same time they develop a reputation of truly having their employees' best interests at heart.

Bill Bufe, Plante & Moran's Human Resources Director, joined the company directly out of college with a major in accounting. He started as an auditor, but it wasn't long before he realized he had a knack for recruiting and training. As he expressed interest in this area, he found his responsibilities gradually shifting. Over time he moved from audit partner to human resources. His responsibilities changed as his interests changed. Thirty-two years later, he is still with the company because he knows he is valued. Employees know the management at Plante & Moran wants them to do what they love and what they do best. It is one of the ways the management demonstrates that employees are important. It is one of the ways they provide inherent recognition.

Because the average employee changes jobs every few years, managers typically feel less of an obligation to provide growth opportunities to their employees than did their predecessors a few decades ago. Ironically, one of the reasons people leave is to pursue new growth opportunities. If managers focused more attention on creating new opportunities for their employees, they could reduce turnover and increase inherent recognition.

To improve both retention and enthusiasm, help employees take on new and different responsibilities. Recognize employees' value to the organization by giving them opportunities to grow and learn. Invest your time and budget in helping employees develop skills that will move them forward in their careers—even if your department won't benefit directly from those skills. The more opportunities for growth that you provide, the greater your reputation for developing people. You will attract people who particularly value this form of recognition—people who will work hard to make your department successful.

Pay and Benefits

Pay and benefits demonstrate individual value. Pay people less than they're worth and less than others in similar positions are paid, and they will interpret that to mean, "You don't matter to us."

Underpaying Employees

A CEO once asked me to help implement a recognition program to address a problem his company was having. The problem? This company had 300 percent turnover!

The first question I asked was "What is causing this kind of turnover?" I didn't have to dig too deep to find the answer. They were paying employees far less than the industry average. In fact, 75 percent of those working elsewhere were making more than they were.

No corporate recognition program was going to undo the message that was inherent in being significantly underpaid.

Underpaid employees feel exploited. Common benefits such as health insurance and vacation have an impact similar to fair pay. Provide less than is customary, and employees feel undervalued. According to Frederick Herzberg,[3] pay and benefits don't motivate, but their lack can cause dissatisfaction. In the same regard, people really don't think of pay and benefits as recognition, but they can see their absence as a lack of recognition.

As a manager, you probably don't have a great deal of say in how much your group, as a whole, is paid. If your group is paid well or has outstanding benefits, talk to employees about how they are valued by both you and the organization. If they are underpaid or have limited benefits, you need to counteract the negative impact by explaining the situation as best you can. Maybe your company is going through hard times, and the situation is temporary. Maybe your company simply doesn't think that it has to meet industry standards. Whatever the reason, clarify that you think they are worth more than they are getting.

Work Environment

Do employees have the resources they need to do their work? Is their work area clean and safe? The work environment that you help create is another way that you tell employees that they are valued. Like pay and benefits, it's not so much that they see these things as recognition; rather, they see a poor work environment as a lack of recognition of their value to you and the organization. Employees don't say, "Golly, I have all this information at my disposal; they must think I'm important." They don't spend much time thinking about the work environment—unless it's substandard. Then employees begin to question their importance to the organization. Public school teachers offer a classic example. Many teachers dig into their own paychecks to buy basic classroom supplies like paper and markers. When they have to do this, they're likely to think, "The district [or community] doesn't consider my work important." Is it any wonder many teachers feel undervalued?

Many elements of the work environment are out of a manager's control. School principals may have no budget for supplies, but that doesn't mean they can't work with parents, teachers, and community supporters to find a solution. Fire and police chiefs can't guarantee a work environment that is always safe. They can, however, work with their people to create as safe an environment as possible. Anything a manager does to improve the employee work environment—successful or not—will recognize employee value.

One element of the work environment is within a manager's control. Every manager can influence team spirit. Managers are the primary influence as to whether the work environment is oppressive or supportive. To create a more positive environment, you can introduce humor into the workday, have small celebrations, and encourage people to work together. People will enjoy being part of your group and will feel valued. They will recognize that you have their best interests in mind.

Recognition Is Everywhere

Anything that tells people they are valued and important has inherent recognition. It isn't all about perks and special benefits. It's about basic respect. A sixth-grade teacher told me that when he experienced a hearing loss, his principal refused to do anything to help him remain effective. Her indifference and lack of support showed him he wasn't valued. Ultimately, he resigned.

Recognition, or lack of it, really is inherent in everything we do. Keeping employees informed and updated recognizes their value. Providing the best possible work environment does the same thing. Consider the Plante & Moran philosophy: managers believe they should rerecruit their employees every day. Bill Bufe describes rerecruiting this way: "Think of your best staff member. Think as if he is coming in to see you today. What would you do or say if he said he was leaving? Do those things anyway."

TAKING ACTION

- Provide appropriate opportunities. While you are delegating responsibilities, consider who has the appropriate skills *and* who would value a new opportunity.
- Clarify your organization's purpose, and make sure employees understand their role in achieving that purpose.
- Provide the tools, resources, and information employees need to do their jobs effectively.
- Treat employees as if they have just said they are leaving. What will you do differently in order to keep them?

chapter **3**

Recognition Starts with Your Relationships

What is it that makes recognition work? That's what I wanted to know when I began asking employees from around the country to tell me about memorable workplace recognition they had received. I wanted to hear directly from the people being recognized and get their reaction to their employers' recognition efforts. I wanted to hear about the recognition experiences that had "made their day."

In my initial research, I solicited the opinions of over one hundred employees across the United States. My continuing research has expanded to over a thousand and includes people from all over the world.

So, what do employees say makes their day?

Sticky Recognition

If your manager put a sticker on a report you had written, would that make an impression on you? Would that

36

impression be positive or negative? Two women from two different companies each described having a sticker applied to a report that they had prepared. The stickers made a big impression. Each woman said that she would never forget how it felt to receive one. That's where the similarity ends. One described the sticker as an example of the types of silly things her manager does to motivate people. She and her coworkers thought the stickers were childish and embarrassing, an example of recognition with a negative impact. Their negative response might seem like the only reasonable reaction to receiving a sticker, except that the other woman told the story as an example of recognition with a positive impact. She said the stickers were highly valued in her company. They were both meaningful and memorable. Getting a sticker showed that your work was of exceptional quality. It was a little like getting a Pulitzer Prize.

Makes you want to shop at the second sticker store, doesn't it? If only it were that simple. Clearly, the form that recognition takes isn't what creates the impact. It isn't the quality of the sticker, nor is it simply a matter of difference in individual preference. If these women are representing their organizations in a fairly accurate manner, they share their opinions with the majority of their coworkers. So what is the difference? What makes one sticker valuable and the other absurd?

Further exploration of the sticker stories revealed a difference in the relationships that these two women had with the managers presenting the stickers. The "Pulitzer" manager was highly regarded and had an excellent relationship with his employees. Any form of recognition he used, from candy bars to public praise, would probably have positive results. The other manager had never earned employee respect. Any form of recognition he used, including bonuses and promotions, would probably have failed. Employees would have viewed them with suspicion.

Everything Else Is Secondary

With recognition, nothing is more important than the relationship between the giver and the receiver. You can structure an innovative and generous program. You can offer frequent, timely, and proportional recognition. You can plan a program that is technically flawless, but none of that matters if the people you are recognizing don't value your feedback. Next to relationships, everything else is secondary.

Managers who are most successful spend less time thinking about recognition itself and more time thinking about how they can help the people they work with.

> **Here are some of the thoughts and actions that will make you successful:**
>
> - Get to know your people.
> - Help others learn and grow.
> - Share information, and trust people to use it appropriately.
> - Value both the individual and his or her contribution.
>
> People can tell when someone really cares about them. That can't be faked. When it comes to recognition that works, nothing can replace sincere respect and the positive relationships that it creates.

Consider your own work relationships. Do people trust you to have their best interests at heart? Whether you are aware of it or not, our colleagues and coworkers keep a kind of mental balance sheet on each of us. Steven Covey calls it an "emotional bank account."[1] I prefer "trust account." When you make a promise and follow through, you make a small deposit into your trust account. When you are honest and open, you make another deposit. Give an evasive answer or make inappropriate disclosures about other employees, and you write a large check. Listen poorly, offer insincere recognition, or represent yourself as an expert when you're not, and before you know it, that trust account is overdrawn, and the people you work with have stamped an imaginary NSF (Not Sufficient Funds) on your forehead. Your account is the reputation you build one person at a time. That reputation decides the quality of your relationships and the impact of your recognition.

If you have any doubts about the relationships you've built, forget about actively recognizing people for a while. Instead, work on the inherent recognition that comes with trust, respect, and caring. You will strengthen the foundation on which your relationships are built. Keep the best interests of employees and coworkers at heart, and the recognition that you offer will have a positive impact.

Employees Have Their Say

A director-level member of a network marketing organization told me that he had competed for his company's President's Circle Award.[2] After a year of hard work, he won. He was the top sales producer for his region. At the annual conference, the president of the company presented him with a plaque. The director was very proud of his accomplishment and the organization-wide recognition that it offered. The experience would have been very positive and motivating, except that when he returned to his seat and looked at the plaque, he discovered that his name had been misspelled. Now he sensed that the award might not be as important to the president as it was to him, but he didn't want to jump to any conclusions. He told the president about the error and gave him the opportunity to make things right. The president could have repaired the situation by simply apologizing and getting the plaque corrected. Instead, he responded, "Oh, well . . . ."

The company president in this story assumed that getting the top sales producer award was what mattered. What he didn't understand was that the director was more interested in how the award would affect their relationship. He assumed that, as the top sales producer, he was now a member of the organization's inner circle. He assumed that he and the president would have a new relationship and that the award was the formal announcement of that relationship to the rest of the organization.

Seeing his name misspelled cast doubt on his assumptions, but he offered the president the opportunity to repair the situation and reconfirm that he valued their relationship. Instead, the president's lack of interest in rectifying the mistake made it clear to the director that their relationship was insignificant. Recognition from the president no longer has meaning for this director. While he may continue to be top sales producer for a while, his sense of loyalty to the organization is damaged. When a new job opportunity comes along, he will be much more likely to take it.

Relationships are the cornerstone of recognition. In interview after interview, this same theme kept replaying itself. Without trust, respect, and communication, recognition doesn't matter. With these things, nearly anything can become valued recognition.

Some respondents told of managers who let them work flexible hours or gave them control over how the work was completed. Others shared how supervisors helped them overcome obstacles, let them find their own way through obstacles, or selected roles for them that offered new and interesting challenges. Not everyone mentioned their managers or supervisors when they told of recognition that made their day. They also told stories of coworkers who shared credit for success on a project or offered appreciation for their assistance. I heard dozens of very different responses to my questions about what makes recognition memorable and meaningful. The common thread throughout was that the person offering the recognition knew the recipient well enough to know what was wanted or needed and then provided it. They had built a respectful relationship.

Respectful Relationships and Recognition

The president of a company asks an employee to take his place on a panel discussion at an international conference.

Result? She says that this opportunity was one that she will never forget. The president was highly respected in his field and with his employees. Without his saying so with words, the employee interpreted his request to mean that he considered her an expert in their field and that he trusted her to represent him. No wonder this opportunity made her day.

If she had a poor relationship with the president, she wouldn't have interpreted the request the same way. She would have wondered why he didn't want to go and why she was stuck taking his place.

A sports fan receives her annual company-required performance evaluation. The written evaluation contains sports terminology to describe her performance. Her supervisor uses phrases like "You really scored big" and "Shows an improved ability to tackle problems."

Result? She feels her supervisor has communicated to her that he cares about both her and her performance. They have a strong relationship built on trust and loyalty.

With a poor relationship, an evaluation like this would have caused the employee to roll her eyes in ridicule.

Filling the Other Guy's Basket

Some organizations seem to have an almost intuitive understanding about workplace relationships. When you enter one of these organizations, you get a sense that everyone likes, trusts, and respects the people they work with. These organizations have a reputation as a great place to work. They have their choice of the best employees in their industries. They have no trouble recruiting or retaining, even while others struggle. They get consistently high job satisfaction ratings from their employees, and employees go out of their way to find ways to improve their products, services, and work environment. Recognition in these organizations reinforces the positive relationships that have already been built.

At Dallas-based retailer The Container Store, 97 percent of employees agree with the survey statement "People care about each other here." The company has made respect for employees a cornerstone of their philosophy. They show that respect in a number of ways. Even with more than forty stores from coast to coast, the executive team still knows most full-time employees by name. Part-timers are known as prime-timers, and employee salaries are well above industry average. Everything they do, individually and as an organization, is meant to acknowledge the vital role that all employees play in the success of the company.

Ranked on *Fortune* magazine's "100 Best Companies to Work For" list year after year, The Container Store rates consistently high in employee satisfaction. It has a turnover rate of about 15 percent in an industry where annual turnover of over 100 percent is common, and more than 40 percent of new hires come from employee referrals. Reduced costs associated with recruiting and hiring mean the company is able to pay higher salaries than the industry average and still experience 15 to 20 percent sales growth each year.

At The Container Store, employees believe that everyone should "fill the other guy's basket to the brim." It's a memorable image for a retailer, one that suggests that everyone is responsible for making sure that both customers and coworkers get what they need. Employees live this philosophy. Elizabeth Barrett, VP of Operations, shared an example that illustrates this philosophy. A customer forgot her merchandise in the parking lot of one of their stores and later returned to retrieve it. When she found that it wasn't in the parking lot, she went into the store to see if it had been turned in. The customer was very upset to discover that it hadn't been. The employee whom she spoke with assessed the situation and literally "filled her basket to the brim," replacing the missing merchandise.

Make sure people get what they need. This philosophy doesn't mean that The Container Store employees give away the store, but it does mean that they take care of the customers and each other. Employees fill their coworkers' baskets to the brim in a variety of ways. They might grab a ladder from the stockroom for someone who is struggling with a ladder that is too small or fill in for someone who has to take a day off unexpectedly. You'll often overhear employees in all areas of the company saying, "Thanks for filling my basket!" It is all about helping one another any way that they can.

The Container Store does a good job of demonstrating that, while relationships are between individuals, organizational structure and culture can also work to build relationships. The company has developed a culture that puts relationships first. The leadership sets a strong example, and managers and employees follow that example because they firmly believe in the philosophy. According to Jane Ellen Graham, Travel Manager, "I have never worked anywhere else where I felt appreciated every day! It is so nice to have people take the time to say thanks even

Organizational Respect

The executive team at The Container Store leads the way in living this philosophy. They are continually looking for new ways to fill employees' baskets to the brim. The following are just a few of the ways they have done so:

- **They made the decision to "blow up HR,"** giving many of its responsibilities back to each store in order to strengthen the relationship between employees and their managers. They wanted employees to bring issues directly to their managers rather than to an intermediary.
- **Full-time store employees receive a minimum of 241 hours of training in their first year!** That is 11 percent of a standard forty-hour work week. In subsequent years, training averages out to approximately 162 hours per year.
- **All full-time employees were granted their wish to have two consecutive days off.** This practice is unusual in retail and is particularly surprising given that a full third of all Container Store employees are full-time.

though I'm just doing my job. It makes you want to always make the extra effort, because your fellow employees will do the same for you." Everyone in this company fills the other guy's basket with respect and recognition.

Creating Loyalty

The low turnover and solid growth rate at The Container Store demonstrate that strong relationships create a tremendous amount of employee loyalty. The correlation between turnover, relationship, and loyalty isn't unique to The Container Store. Most companies that put a high value on relationships enjoy a correspondingly high level of employee loyalty. Xilinx, a semiconductor company based in San Jose, California, provides another example.

> To build strong relationships, one of the most important things recognition should do is communicate that a person is valued. Xilinx did this during the economic slump that began in 2001 in a way that employees found particularly meaningful. Although many companies say they value employees and structure elaborate recognition programs to demonstrate that value, when hard times hit, the first thing many do is lay off 25 percent of their workforce. This action sends a conflicting message that damages relationships and causes morale to drop among those employees who remain. Managers at Xilinx, in contrast, decided the best way they could demonstrate employee value was to avoid layoffs if at all possible.
>
> According to Chris Taylor, who was then Senior Director of Human Resources, Xilinx leaders sat down and reassessed their company values. They decided that if they really respected people and really believed their people were their best resource, they should recognize that fact by finding alternate ways to scale back labor costs, reserving layoffs as their last resort.
>
> The year 2001 was a tough one for most technology companies. Xilinx was no exception. By December, revenue was off 50 percent. What made Xilinx exceptional under these circumstances was that the company hadn't laid off a single employee. It could have chosen a more cost-effective short-term solution, but management believed that the long-term gain from having retained their highly valuable workforce was worth the risk. Xilinx found other ways to reduce labor costs. Management started with a tiered pay cut, with the biggest earners taking the largest cut. Then

came an across-the-board pay cut, and finally a variety of voluntary programs to decrease labor costs. They communicated their plans to employees each step of the way, never promising that layoffs wouldn't eventually become necessary, but demonstrating that layoffs would be the last resort. This commitment to Xilinx employees was a powerful form of recognition.

> *Management demonstrated just how*
> *valued their employees were.*

Employees responded with a tremendous amount of understanding and loyalty. Some offered to take even greater pay cuts than requested. The organization demonstrated employee value in a way that no recognition program could match. Through their commitment to retaining their people, even during difficult times, the leadership strengthened their relationship with every employee.

A strong relationship between employees and the leadership is nothing new at Xilinx. When CEO Wim Roelandts left Hewlett-Packard to join the firm in 1996, Xilinx was heading into a difficult time. Under his leadership, the company was able to gain momentum, surpassing its closest competitor in revenue. During the fiscal year that ended March 2000, Xilinx reached a milestone: it hit the billion-dollar mark. To show his gratitude, Roelandts gave every employee a bottle of champagne labeled Xilinx Billion Dollars. It came in a champagne bucket engraved with the individual's name. It was a nice gift, and because recognition goes both ways, employees wanted to thank him for his leadership. They decided to take out a full-page ad that read, "Wim Roelandts: Thanks a Billion for Your Leadership!" Behind the bold-print headline, in faint print was the name of every employee in the organization. When employees showed their CEO the ad at a company meeting, there was a five-minute standing ovation. Roelandts was choked up. Even CEOs love recognition.

Strong bonds between employees at all levels create powerful company loyalty. Building strong bonds means building trust. Building trust means developing respect and cooperation. In organizations where strong relationships are valued, everyone works hard to maintain these things and is careful not to do anything to damage those relationships.

Creating a Respectful Environment

So, what do you do, as a manager, if you don't work for a Xilinx or a Container Store? You don't have control over how your organization behaves, but you can replicate their philosophies relating to respectful relationships.

- ☑ Be on the lookout for anything in your organization that seems disrespectful of employees. Do what you can to encourage change or, at the least, lessen the impact on your employees.
- ☑ Ask employees what they want and need that will make them most effective.
- ☑ Listen and respond to the best of your ability.
- ☑ Encourage respectful behavior among team members.
- ☑ Become a proponent of company policies that serve both the employees and the organization.

How Do You Measure Up?

Do you focus on what matters most? Ask yourself whether the people you work with value the recognition that you already

give. Have you developed mutual trust, respect, and loyalty
with them? If you aren't sure, ask them or participate in a multirater assessment (often referred to as a 360 assessment) of
your skills as a manager. You can also use the simple relationship self-assessment tool available on the Make Their Day website (www.maketheirday.com/1minute-assessment.pdf).

The Dangers of Intracompany Competition

Lots of organizations, divisions, and departments stage competitions. After all, contests among departments, teams, and individuals seem like a fun way to achieve a goal. Sports pit teams
against each other, and people enjoy the competition, so why not
enjoy that same spirit of competition at work? The difference is
that in sports, opposing teams aren't expected to work together
or cooperate and collaborate after the competition. High-stakes
competition often creates animosity between competitors, which
damages relationships and makes working together difficult.
Consider the following situation:

> A small manufacturer of bath products holds a produc-
> tion contest. The morning and evening shifts compete to
> see who produces the most during the quarter. The prize
> is a $300 bonus for everyone on the production shift: line
> workers, members of the maintenance crew, and the shift
> supervisor. At the end of the first week, production is up.
> Line workers are working faster and smarter. Changes to
> the line that will improve performance are suggested. So
> far so good.
>
> As the second week comes to a close, management
> learns that production levels have stalled. They give both
> shifts a pep talk, trying to motivate them to find innova-

tive ways to increase production. Workers push for ways to outpace their competitors. They skip routine maintenance, withhold information, hoard supplies, and do their best to make production impossible for the other crew. Cooperation that once existed is now gone. Nobody wins.

You can have successful intracompany competitions without damaging relationships, but only if you work hard to ensure that those relationships remain intact. Competition has to be secondary to maintaining the bonds between employees. Focus on what matters most. The tips in the next box will help.

Competitions That Work

It's possible to compete successfully without damaging relationships if you do a couple of things differently.

- Don't compete for high-stake rewards. Keep competitions fun by keeping the prizes fun. People aren't as likely to toss out the relationships that they've built for a pizza party as they are for a $300 bonus.
- Compete to surpass past measures, such as improving on a safety record, beating a sales goal, or improving a customer satisfaction rating. Multiple winners should be possible.

Recognition that works has more to do with trust, respect, loyalty, and creating strong relationships than contests, programs, or awards. Without healthy working relationships, recognition is meaningless. It is up to you to create an atmosphere of trust, respect, and loyalty where recognition can thrive.

TAKING ACTION

- Assess your relationships with the people you work with. If your relationships are damaged, recognition will be meaningless. Build strong relationships first, and then you can explore other ways to recognize people.
- Look at how your organization demonstrates the value of relationships. See if there are ways that you can build trust and respect into the organizational culture. If you're unable to influence organizational behavior any other way, work to improve the relationships within your department or unit. Model behavior that creates strong working relationships.
- Regardless of your role in your organization, you can show recognition by treating individuals as the valuable people they are. Find ways to help others. As The Container Store employees would say, "Fill their baskets to the brim."

2

Whose Job Is Recognition, Anyway?

4

Managing for the Greatest Impact

Right in the middle of facilitating a workshop, I say, "James, in preparing for this workshop, I looked through the usage data for the company's recognition program. I noticed that you have really embraced this program and have the highest program usage. Tell us, has it made any difference with your employees?"

This wasn't a setup. I hadn't spoken with James ahead of time. From experience I didn't see asking this question as a risky move. I fully expected a positive response. That is why his hesitant-sounding "Yeah . . . ." took me by surprise. I held my breath as he looked around the room. "What is said here stays here, right?" he asked his fellow managers. They nodded. "Well, there is one employee. . . ." Looks of recognition appeared on the faces of the other managers in the room. They knew all about the "one employee," and none of it was good. "With this employee . . . ," he said, "the change has been *phenomenal*."

Whew! Nothing like adding a little drama to a workshop! While I recovered, he explained that the difference in attitude and behavior was so extraordinary that he was afraid to jinx it by mentioning that it had ever been anything but stellar.

What had this manager done that caused such a turnaround? He had simply offered a little specific praise on a few occasions, and, in his words, the change was "phenomenal."

This story illustrates what you can experience over and over again, by effectively using recognition: that the manager really does have a powerful impact on employee morale and productivity.

The Most Important Role

A university employee explains the power of the manager making a personal connection. "The new dean sent me a birthday card with a handwritten note. I don't think I've had a boss do that in my professional life. Maybe a boss has added their name to a card from the staff, maybe they've said 'Happy Birthday' when they've seen balloons or cards at my desk, or maybe they chipped in for a gift. But to have a boss with far too many direct reports make a point of sending a card with a note was surprisingly touching. Such a small thing had such a big impact."

Ask one hundred employees what their favorite form of recognition is, and you will get at least fifty different answers. Ask the same one hundred employees *who* they most want to receive recognition from, and the majority will say they want it from their manager or supervisor.

Recognition from all sources is important, but it doesn't carry the same weight as recognition that comes from the manager. In fact, my research shows that *70 percent of the most meaningful recognition comes from a manager.*[1] Seems unlikely that you can achieve high satisfaction without manager involvement, doesn't it?

The 50/30/20 Rule

Employees want recognition from a number of sources. They need it to come from their manager. They also want it to come from the organization, in the form of inherent recognition and big awards. And, finally, they expect it to come from their peers both formally and informally.

There seems to be a preferred mix for these three sources: manager, peer, and organization. Overall, employees want about 20 percent of recognition to come from the organization, 30 percent from their peers, and a full 50 percent from their managers. Fifty percent manager, 30 percent peer, 20 percent organization—this combination is the 50/30/20 Rule.

I often hear from managers who want to address employees' need for recognition through peer programs. Peer programs are important, but if managers successfully distance themselves from the recognition process and ignore the 50/30/20 Rule, employees will be frustrated by the lack of manager recognition.

Here is an example of the 50/30/20 Rule: Athleta is a women's sportswear company that was a start-up when described in the first edition. It was featured for the inherent recognition the company provided by trusting employees and offering them a great deal of autonomy.

In 2003, the inherent recognition provided was so compelling that the company only experienced about

5 percent turnover each year. Yet, at that time, according to Rick Scott who was Director of Team Support, many forms of recognition were missing at Athleta. He said that few managers coached or trained employees or worked to provide them with appropriate new opportunities. He told me he believed that managers did little to specifically address the recognition needs of employees. They were virtually ignoring 50 percent of the preferred mix—the recognition that comes from the manager.

A 2002 survey of Athleta employees showed less than 50 percent satisfaction with recognition overall. Although the organizational culture and the support of both leadership and peers provided recognition, the missing component was recognition that comes from an employee's manager or supervisor. The survey confirmed what senior management suspected. They needed to train managers and supervisors to better meet their employees' recognition needs. In doing so, they would work to address the preferred mix of recognition sources.

The Manager's Opportunity and Responsibility

As a manager or supervisor, you are most able to provide the recognition that employees crave. Recognition that you offer reassures employees that they are performing up to expectations. According to an employee of a large health care provider, "Recognition from my manager is most important because he's the one doing my annual review, not the organization or my coworkers. He's the one likely to recommend me for a promotion." Even those who say they prefer peer recognition see it, at least in part, as a way to secure recognition from management.

As one employee stated, "The praise of coworkers can sometimes lead to praise from management. If management is listening, then they will hear your coworkers sing your praises and perhaps look at you in a different light."

As a manager or supervisor, you have the greatest opportunity and responsibility for providing employee recognition.

Opportunity

No one is in a better position to offer consistent, meaningful recognition than the employee's manager or supervisor. If you are in this role, you have knowledge and opportunities that others just don't have.

You should have

☐ The most comprehensive information on what employees are accomplishing.

☐ Access to any recognition budget that is available.

☐ An opportunity to learn about how each employee wants to be recognized.

☐ Knowledge about whether employees are receiving frequent, timely, and appropriate recognition from all sources combined.

☐ The opportunity to coach employees on how to provide self-recognition (see Chapter 8).

☐ The ear of upper management. Managers and supervisors can recognize employees in a way that improves employees' visibility and increases their chances of promotion.

☐ A high-profile role in your department or division, putting you in the best position to model good recognition behavior and encourage peer recognition.

Responsibility

As a manager, you represent the organization. Particularly in large organizations, employees tend to blur the distinction between manager and organization. A study by Maritz Research[2] found a strong correlation between employee support for the company's products and services and their perception of their managers. One question in the study asked employees if their managers "walk the talk." The other asked if employees support their company's products and services. Ninety percent of the employees who responded that their managers do walk the talk also expressed support for their company's products and services. Of those who answered that their managers do not walk the talk, only 25 percent expressed support for the company's products and services. In the eyes of employees, the manager is the organization. If managers don't recognize employees, most employees will say that the organization, in general, doesn't recognize them.

Missed Opportunity

Managers and supervisors have the opportunity and means to create recognition that offers the greatest impact. Yet, almost half of all managers fail to provide any meaningful recognition. Most managers know that their employees want more recognition, yet they resist for a variety of reasons. Compare the list that follows to your own concerns.

- **They resist because they believe that being paid is the only recognition employees need.** In their view, employees are motivated by money. They think recognition isn't necessary and can lead employees to expect more money. The truth is employees want recognition for its own sake. In a preference survey conducted in 2008, respondents preferred recognition over a bonus or incentive.[3]

- **They resist because they are too busy doing their job to spend time on recognition.** Managers and supervisors have too much to do. Adding recognition to their to-do list adds to the workload. This viewpoint is accurate yet also shortsighted. Employees who receive regular, quality recognition are more productive and self-directed. Employees who feel recognized make the manager's job easier, not harder.

- **They resist because they are afraid they will be accused of playing favorites.** Favoritism is a very real concern that can be addressed, in part, by establishing sound criteria and then consistently recognizing employees for progress in meeting those criteria. (See Chapter 13 for more on fairness.)

- **They resist because they have experienced a program that failed miserably.** Many managers and supervisors have participated in recognition programs that were so poorly received they are reluctant to try again. Without getting into all the reasons why programs succeed or fail, I want to emphasize that recognition doesn't come from programs; it comes from people. A manager's or supervisor's personal efforts to recognize employees will produce better results than any program.

- **They resist because their own attempts at recognition have failed.** Managers and supervisors who don't understand what it takes to provide meaningful recognition are likely to get a response similar to this firsthand account from a workshop participant:

> "Twice our director gave out certificates of appreciation. I put both of mine in the recycling at home. He gave everyone the same certificate. I felt they didn't mean anything because he gave them to all 140 employees in the unit, including the person who doesn't perform most of his duties, the one who comes in late and leaves early nearly every day, and another who spends most of her time on the phone on personal business."

The only thing this manager recognized was that
these were the people on his unit's payroll.

He doesn't understand that recognition must be tied to performance and the value that each employee provides to the unit. In his attempt to be fair, he was unfair to those who work hard and act responsibly. After a few lackluster attempts, this manager will probably decide recognition doesn't work and quit trying. He has missed the opportunity to offer meaningful recognition because he doesn't understand what makes recognition work.

Building on the Relationship Foundation

Employees look to you for feedback on their performance. Well-phrased feedback, whether it is praise or suggestions for improvement, is one of the most basic and valuable forms of recognition you can provide. In the preference survey mentioned earlier in the chapter, 47 percent of employees said they would like to receive feedback *every* week. Preferences do vary according to the number of years in the workforce (those with fewer years want more frequent feedback), but every employee wants some feedback from a caring manager.

Corrective feedback can be recognition. If feedback is offered with good intentions and framed as a development tool, most employees appreciate it. They know that they have to improve and grow in order to progress. If employees seem to resent all corrective feedback, most likely it is because they aren't receiving enough of the positive kind.

Many managers only speak to employees when a problem comes up. To quote one employee, "Positive comments are usually few and far between." If you only offer suggestions for

Corrective Feedback as Recognition

Very early in his career, my husband Gary went to his manager to complain that he had too much work. He told the manager that he didn't have time to get it all done. Knowing that too much work wasn't the problem, his manager could have simply ignored the complaint. Instead, he recognized Gary's value to the organization by demonstrating his commitment to helping Gary improve. He helped Gary improve his own awareness by gently pointing out the numerous times that week that he had seen Gary standing around chatting with coworkers. He suggested that if Gary instead used that time to tackle his outstanding projects, he would be able to finish his work. For the next few weeks, Gary caught himself each time he stopped to chat. Using that time as his manager had suggested, he found that he really was able to finish his work. His effectiveness grew because of his manager's feedback.

improvement and don't recognize what your employees do well, then employees will tune you out. Provide a balance of positive and corrective, and both will be seen as recognition.

Give at least three times more praise than corrective feedback. If that seems like too much, think about the last time you lay awake late at night rehashing something that happened the day before. Were you patting yourself on the back or playing the "could have," "should have," "why did I" game of regret? Most of us quickly forget the positives while replaying our mistakes over and over in our heads. The people who report to you do the same thing. The three-to-one ratio just helps provide balance.

Avoid adding a little dose of corrective feedback to the
praise you offer. The "You were great, but . . ." style of
praise completely cancels out the positive.

What Exceptional Managers Do

In preparing to write the first edition, I asked employees to tell me
about managers who did an exceptional job of recognizing their
people. Employees nominated managers from a variety of organizations. The three managers I selected came from companies with
three diverse approaches to formal recognition: one company had
very little formal recognition, another had formal recognition that
wasn't very effective, and the third had programs that were very
well received. All three stories are still relevant. I believe you will
find it interesting to see how little the existing recognition culture
affects how these three managers approach recognition.

Company 1

Jim Wheeler, an employee at Williams, an energy company in
Tulsa, Oklahoma, suggested that I interview his former manager,
Michelle Boyes. When he worked for Boyes, she was Manager of
Employee Learning and Development and led a team of eighteen
people. According to Wheeler, "She exercised her remarkable talents in selecting and developing talent and facilitating high-per-
formance teamwork in order to take our ragtag bunch and turn
us into a respected group of professionals." Not only did
Wheeler believe that Boyes was a skilled manager, but he also
was impressed by her ability to encourage recognition among the
members of their team. In nominating her, Wheeler wrote:

> "Last year, after some very intensive work over a period
> of months, our entire team got together at a lakeside

cabin. The opportunity to be in a casual setting away from the office with some good food was a reward in and of itself.

"We ate breakfast and discussed the very large project we had just closed out. She gave a token of appreciation to each member of the team and had special prizes for three team members who had been selected by their peers for contributing the most effort.

"The next part of the day was intended to only last an hour or so. Each person on the team would take the hot seat and be 'forced' to listen while other members were invited to say what they most appreciated about what the person brought to the team. It didn't take long to realize that we were going to be there awhile. It took three hours to get through our entire team. Not everyone spoke every time— only those who genuinely had something to say. I'm not usually the 'touchy-feely' type, but when facades dropped and people got real, it was just too good not to enjoy. That will always stand as one of the most memorable events of my life, because it is a rare occasion in anyone's life to be on either the giving or receiving end of such a quality time of recognizing what people contribute."

What kind of manager can make employees who aren't the "touchy-feely" type comfortable with a recognition event that resembles an encounter group? When I interviewed Boyes, I learned that she was a retired army first sergeant who has been awarded numerous prestigious leadership awards. Her background provided plenty of experience with formal recognition programs. Clearly, she also had the opportunity to learn how to give the kind of personalized recognition that Wheeler described.

When I interviewed Boyes, she told me that Williams didn't have an enterprise-wide recognition program. So far, recognition had been left up to individual managers. This approach works as an overall strategy, but only if the manager has a good grasp on what makes recognition effective. Clearly, Boyes is a manager who understands what makes employees feel recognized. She offers these tips to help you offer recognition that works:

Tip 1: Provide clear expectations, validation, respect, loyalty, and trust. Boyes focuses on building strong working relationships with each person because she knows relationships are the foundation for effective recognition.

Tip 2: Figure out what people have to offer, and leverage those strengths. According to Boyes, the key to making people feel recognized is to select challenges and opportunities that are appropriate for and stretch the individual while still focusing on results.

Tip 3: Individualize recognition. Boyes makes sure she knows enough about employees to select recognition that they will value. Individualizing recognition was the key to making the "hot seat" so successful. She knew her team well enough to know that, even with initial reluctance, they would warm up to the idea of taking turns recognizing each other verbally. She uses this same knowledge about what her people value to select recognition awards when appropriate.

Tip 4: Encourage employees to recognize each other. The recognition session at their retreat was only one example of peers recognizing each other. Team members acknowledge each other regularly— whenever they see someone doing something right. Boyes encourages her employees by modeling good behavior and coaching them to be alert for opportunities to recognize each other.

Tip 5: Celebrate as a team. Once a year, Boyes' team has a formal recognition event. Three volunteers put a dinner together that includes some form of fun recognition activity for the group.

Company 2

Another response to my request for the names of managers with exceptional recognition skills came from Bruno Petrauskas. He submitted the name of a manager he had worked for eleven years earlier! Elizabeth Dressner was Petrauskas's manager when he worked as a technical writer for Information Associates, an IT solution provider based in Rochester, New York. Dressner managed a group of twenty-four technical writers. According to Petrauskas, "She was my manager for several years, and she was truly exceptional at making me feel valued, appreciated, and recognized."

It had been eleven years since Petrauskas worked for Dressner, yet when considering the question of exceptional recognition, her name came to mind immediately. How did Dressner create that kind of impact? According to Petrauskas, it was mostly the little things. It was regular gestures of appreciation. "When I would get a 'praise and thanks-for-your-contribution' e-mail from someone, Elizabeth would send me a note to express her own appreciation and praise and then forward both the e-mail and her note to her own manager and the personnel department." She demonstrated to Petrauskas how much she valued having him as a part of her team. "There were a number of times that we had to work extra long hours to get a particular job or project done. One time I had already put in over fifty hours by the middle of the week. I recall Elizabeth coming to my cubicle, taking one look at me (I did look tired and beat), and telling me to go home immediately and rest, not just for that day but the next as well. She really cared about my well-being."

When I interviewed Dressner, I learned that Information Associates had formal recognition programs and that her current company has its programs as well. In Dressner's experience, formal programs don't work that well, regardless of the company. She says they never seem to hit the mark and sometimes even have the opposite result.

Dressner participated on a team that evaluated their formal recognition programs. According to Dressner, the team's findings confirmed that "the efforts of managers are far more effective in terms of employee morale and satisfaction" than are the formal programs that they have in place. She believes, "You can't rely on anyone else to give your folks the recognition that they need."

What tips does Dressner offer on how to make people feel recognized?

Tip 1: Make recognition personal. Face-to-face, Dressner tells people they are doing a great job and that their team wouldn't accomplish what it does without their help. Petrauskas shared that a good reward for him was time off. Dressner helped him accumulate time off in exchange for overtime hours. The arrangement helped them bring projects in on time and allowed Petrauskas to supplement his vacation time for a longer trip. For others, recognition may be time off to do their holiday shopping, tickets to a movie or sporting event, or a certificate for merchandise at the company store or dinner out.

Tip 2: Stay available and visible. Dressner's door is always open, and if she is in her office, employees are always welcome. Much of the time, though, she is out of the office talking with employees.

Tip 3: Arrange departmental recognition events. Dressner's team has regular celebrations, such as lunches a couple of times a month and parties for new software releases. They held their own Academy Awards where everyone received an award. These awards took into account each person's unique role on the team. They presented one person with a pair of handmade gold lamé gloves, the "Golden Fingers Award," because this person had completed a huge typing project without a single typographical error. Another, a team leader, received an oilcan for "oiling the sticky parts of the corporate bureaucracy."

Tip 4: Encourage your team to become involved in community outreach activities. Dressner's team plans and sponsors events that benefit charities. They participate in walkathons. They serve lunch and officiate over bingo games at a nearby senior center. These activities improve team spirit, and the community recognizes and appreciates their efforts.

Company 3

Deb Tacker, an employee at Remedy, the software company mentioned in the introduction, nominated the third manager included in this chapter. Tacker works in a different department, but she had observed that Janet Lewis, a support services manager of sixteen people on two technical support teams, did an excellent job of recognizing her people. Subsequent interviews with two of Lewis's direct reports, both technical support engineers, confirmed Tacker's observations. Valerie Ford told me that Lewis "goes out of her way to recognize the little things. You don't have to save a big account in order to hear from her." Lisa Murray shared that Lewis "recognizes my capabilities even more than I do myself. She talks with me about where I am and where I want to be. She points out strengths and makes suggestions for new directions."

Remedy Support Services does an excellent job of recognizing employees. Employees get regular visits from the Cookie Lady, who comes to their offices and bakes fresh cookies. There is an Employee Appreciation Week as well as quarterly campaigns tied to fun themes and goals. One campaign to raise customer survey scores to a level that many managers had doubted was possible ended with a chicken-themed celebration ("Management was 'chicken,' but we knew we could do it!"), complete with chicken barbecue, an egg drop contest, and a presentation where the managers did the chicken dance. To top it off, their VP, Mike Little, also affectionately known as Chicken Little, dressed up in a chicken costume. These kinds of activities won't fit into every organization's culture, but the people in Remedy Support Services think they are a perfect fit and say they offer a solid foundation for the recognition that managers offer.

What does a manager do, in an atmosphere such as this, to make direct reports feel even more valued? In Lewis's case, she does many of the same things as the other managers described in this chapter. Lewis makes a point of remembering that what motivates one person won't necessarily motivate another. Like Boyes, she provides challenges that are achievable but at the same time provide an opportunity for growth. Like Dressner, she makes herself available and provides focused attention.

Lewis also encourages employees to create their own recognition. One of her direct reports came up with an idea for peer recognition. Michael Fahrenbruch felt that the engineers knew better than anyone else the achievements their peers had made, and he suggested a program he called "Kudos for Kolleagues." Lewis was enthusiastic, so when another engineer wanted to develop the idea and work with her peers to set the criteria and implement the program, Lewis encouraged her. Now engineers use Kudos for Kolleagues to recognize each other for a variety of things, from helping them fix their telephone headset to volunteering to take the early shift.

Lewis makes the following suggestions on how you can provide valued recognition:

Tip 1: Give instant feedback. When Lewis gets positive feedback about an employee, she adds her positive comments and forwards both to the employee. She says that "little recognition" means as much or more than "big recognition."

Tip 2: Engineer "easy wins." This suggestion doesn't mean give employees easy tasks. Provide achievable challenges that people are passionate about delivering. Then give them the help that they need to deliver.

Tip 3: Motivate the team to recognize each other. Lewis asks her teams to set quarterly goals for the number of Kudos for Kolleagues that they will give each other. She says they never have trouble exceeding that goal.

Tip 4: Hold one-on-one meetings. Lewis meets with every employee each quarter. She makes a point of telling top performers that their contribution is key. She says it's important that these people know that you don't take them for granted.

Going It Alone

There are no big secrets to what you, as a manager or supervisor, can do to make employees feel recognized. It comes down to the basics of really knowing the people who work for you, challenging them to do their best, providing quality feedback, and then recognizing them for their achievements. It is easier when your organization supports your recognition efforts. But if they don't, still do the same things, and you'll still have a positive impact. Without organizational support, you will most likely have to work within a very limited budget, but as you have seen, effective recognition doesn't necessarily require a lot of money.

By paying attention to recognition preferences, offering flexibility and opportunity, and praising and celebrating both individual and team success, you can significantly increase the job satisfaction of the people who work for you. When you begin to get results, in terms of both higher employee retention and increased productivity, you will most likely find that senior management will be more supportive and willing to budget for recognition.

Even if the organization never supports your recognition efforts, you will still be effective if you focus on the basics. To quote one employee who was asked whom he wanted recognition from, "My vote is still with the line supervisor or manager who brings in a case of pop at break time on a hot day . . . that's a tough act for any organization to beat."

TAKING ACTION

- Keep it simple. You can begin by recognizing both the individuals and teams who work directly for you and by acknowledging others when their work affects your group. Offer thanks and praise. Send e-mails, mention results face-to-face, and send a handwritten note occasionally. Look for ways to increase inherent recognition. Develop people by providing appropriate opportunities. Demonstrate that your employees are a valued part of your team.
- Keep it coming. Frequent recognition is more important than grand gestures. Employees said that recognition from managers was about the everyday little things that they did to demonstrate the employees' value to them. To get into the habit of offering frequent recognition, start by finding something positive to recognize about each person at least once each month. As you become more proficient, work toward making sure that your people are recognized at least once per week.
- Reassess your role in the recognition process. You will want to read the chapters about the role of organizational leaders, HR, and individual contributors. You will learn how you can partner with others to create the best recognition experience.

chapter 5

Leading with Vision, Visibility, and Momentum

Everyone can be a leader, whether as a CEO or a team leader. This chapter focuses on the senior leaders within an organization but also looks at what anyone in leadership can do to create a culture of recognition.

Leaders play a unique role in the recognition process. Just as they determine the direction of an organization, department, or project, they can influence the direction of recognition.

The visibility and influence of the people on your executive team make them some of the most potentially effective proponents of recognition within your organization. From their small, personal gestures, to the recognition programs that they personally champion, these executives can set the tone for recognition. If they value recognition, then it's much more likely that everyone within your organization will value it as well. This is because the members of your executive team are in the best *position* to weave recognition into the fiber of the organization. At the same time, regardless of your role, you can offer recognition leadership. Let's look at a few examples.

Developing a Recognition Culture

Some leaders focus on the recognition that is inherent in the workplace, working to ensure that their employees receive recognition directly from the work environment. They create an organizational culture focused on mutual respect, opportunity, and pride. This is true at Design Octaves, Inc., a small manufacturing firm with less than one hundred employees. I consulted with Design Octaves for a number of years and have observed firsthand how Norm Weiss, company president, ensures that his employees feel recognized.

Design Octaves has only one formal recognition program. After ten years of service, Weiss recognizes employees with a trip to Hawaii. At one time, the company also had an Employee of the Month Award, but Weiss chose to discontinue it. Instead, he spends his time ensuring that employees feel valued and respected.

When I first began consulting with Design Octaves, something happened that clearly illustrated that powerful recognition can come simply from the way employees are treated. I was brought into Design Octaves to oversee a project that typically would take a few months to complete. I observed that employees throughout the company were upbeat, loyal, hardworking, and productive. I took this behavior as a good sign. Employees with this kind of positive attitude and commitment would help ensure that the project would go smoothly, and we would finish quickly.

It wasn't long before I knew that the project I had been hired to oversee would become one of the longer and more time-consuming projects I had ever done. It wasn't that the project itself was anything out of the ordinary or that the people weren't motivated. The lack of productivity occurred because the people on my team had absolutely no experience in doing the kind of work that I needed them to do. The lack of experienced team members quickly made this an expensive project for the client.

What happened next showed me how powerful inherent recognition can be. When I went to Weiss and described the problem, I expected that he would want to hire someone with experience to join this team. That would have been the most cost-effective solution. I was surprised to discover that Weiss was already aware that we were proceeding at a fraction of the pace of a more experienced team. That was all right with him. He was more than willing to pay the extra money in order to train his people. He believed that they were worth investing in. The employees on this team knew he had cheaper options, and they knew he was committed to their growth.

Knowing the level of commitment Weiss had to them, these employees felt the same kind of commitment to him. They knew that what he offered was real recognition. It was recognition that said, "You are important," "What you do is important to me," and "I will help you become even more important to the company by providing you with new opportunities." The money Weiss spent to train members of his "family," when he clearly could have recruited more qualified people, had a lasting impact on these employees.

Not much has changed at Design Octaves over the years. Every morning Weiss grabs a cup of coffee and then heads out to the factory floor. He hugs people, shakes their hands, and calls them by name. He says, "I try to make some sort of contact with every person every day. They know that I'm there, that I see them, and that I recognize them."

The respect Weiss shows employees sets the tone throughout the organization. He models what recognition at Design Octaves should look like, and employees follow his lead. Everyone is highly respectful of everyone else, and they all look for ways to assist each other. They recognize the value of every member of their team and work together to provide the kind of workplace where commitment and loyalty are prevalent and turnover is less than 2 percent a year.

Weiss provides leadership by modeling a recognition strategy that focuses on mutual respect. He sets the tone for a company culture that offers inherent recognition. Compare that to this food-processing company, as described by a former employee:

> "I worked at a company that was outwardly hip and socially responsible. They talked about shared goals and values. We created mission, vision, and values in a series of company-wide meetings. We were told that we were responsible for keeping the company true to our values and goals. But it was a crazy-making situation because upper management repeatedly violated core values and failed to provide the resources to implement very important goals around safety, working conditions, and customer complaints."

It seemed as though the leaders of this organization wanted to create a workplace that provided inherent recognition. They told employees they were responsible for creating their own environment. If employees had been able to create their own environment, they would have felt recognized for their trustworthiness, competency, and ability to direct themselves. Instead, when the executive team sabotaged their efforts at every step, they felt betrayed. Unfortunately, this happens in far too many organizations. The members of the executive team generally know what needs to happen and say the words that they know employees want to hear, but then, through their actions, demonstrate that they really didn't mean what they said.

If you are not in senior leadership, if you are a manager, a line supervisor, or a team or project lead, you can still influence the culture of your group. Take a cue from Weiss: connect with every employee, every day. Develop a vision, and then work to live that vision. Look out for the welfare of your people. Creating inherent recognition isn't difficult.

Showing Value through Action

How do you demonstrate that people are valued? What you believe comes through, first and foremost, in your actions. When it comes to recognition, do you

- Take a hands-off approach and decide that recognition is someone else's responsibility?
- Declare that recognition needs to happen and then stand back and wait?
- Roll up your sleeves and lead the way with your actions?

As a leader, the more willing you are to offer recognition, the more likely that others will follow your example. Because of your visibility, you are in an excellent position to model how important recognition is. When managers and employees see their leaders recognizing people, they're more inclined to see the value in offering recognition and are more likely to offer it themselves.

Gestures of recognition that come from the senior leadership of an organization can have a very big impact, no matter how small the gesture. When I asked employees about recognition that had made their day, several described a time when their vice president stopped by their cubicle to chat. During their conversations, each of these employees discovered that the VP knew something about the work they were doing. That simple awareness was meaningful recognition. It was powerful because most employees, especially in larger organizations, don't expect personal attention from senior leaders.

In a workshop years ago, a manager told this story: "I travel a lot and consequently have experienced a lot of flight delays. During a delay on American Airlines, I got to talking to the passenger seated next to me. It turned out that the guy worked for American Airlines and was somehow involved in the repair of the planes. He went on to tell me that the last time he was on a delayed flight, the cause of the delay was fuel leaking from the jet. After a flight crew (not American Airlines) examined the plane, they determined that it required a part that would take four hours to arrive. Four hours. This was the only flight out that day, and a four-hour delay would cause nearly everyone on board to miss connecting flights. The captain came back to ask this off-duty employee if he would please check out the problem. Even though he was dressed in a suit, he went to check it out. Soon he discovered that the problem was a simple gasket. It was quickly fixed, and the flight was on its way.

"The airline employee didn't tell me this just to brag about how dedicated he was. Rather, he was impressed by something else. It turned out that the pilot had sent a letter to the president of American Airlines. The president then sent a letter to the employee, thanking him for his dedication and extending a personal invitation. The employee seated next to me, telling me his story, was now on his way to have dinner with the president and his wife."

Another example of the power of personal attention from the executive team comes from Griffin Hospital, a company that has made *Fortune*'s "100 Best Companies to Work For" list nine years in a row.

Griffin Hospital President and CEO Patrick Charmel kicks off a five-day orientation for new employees and volunteers with a two-hour introduction. Vice presidents and directors lead var-

ious segments of the program. The week is crammed full of valuable information about the hospital and its service philosophy.

> Initially, when the three senior executives began doing
> this orientation, it was a one-day program. They expected
> that the knowledge that employees and volunteers gained
> would be what they valued most. Instead, according to
> Vice President Bill Powanda, employees and volunteers
> said that what they valued most about the orientation
> was "that the three senior executives spent the day with
> us." When Wendy Silver, a registered nurse, went through
> orientation, she said, "I was impressed that the CEO
> spoke for two hours about the hospital's values and cus-
> tomer service focus to educate new employees." Quality
> Manager Deborah Gibber said, "I felt truly welcomed
> and valued." Employees and volunteers know that the
> executives' time is limited, and they are impressed that
> this team would choose to spend their time sharing infor-
> mation and getting to know them. The people who work
> at Griffin Health know they are important from the
> moment they are hired.

Personal attention from the executive team can be powerful,
but the leadership at Griffin Health knows that recognition needs
to come from many different fronts. Although they don't really
think of it this way, they have worked to create an environment
that contains inherent recognition. Griffin Health has a terrific reputation and is best known for its remarkable, almost fanatical customer service. The service is so exceptional that, to date, more than
650 hospitals have visited Griffin Health to learn more about how
staff does it. The hospital's reputation offers significant inherent
recognition. Employees have a tremendous amount of pride in the
quality of their service. The exceptional level of customer service is
also significant because when customers feel important, it's a good
indicator that employees also feel important. Quality service rarely

comes from employees who feel undervalued. The environment at Griffin Health attracts the best people in the industry. The hospital gets around forty applications for every open position! Top physicians want to work there, and the hospital has a low turnover among its nurses—almost unheard of in the health care industry.

Again, if you aren't a senior leader you can still affect pride in the workplace, service, and more just by offering your attention and providing leadership.

Leading Recognition Programs

The Graduate Management Admission Council (GMAC®) of McLean, Virginia, has an on-the-spot recognition program. It is a program structured for both peer- and manager-driven recognition. Brian Maggio, Associate Director of Technology Operations, is a frequent provider of these awards and encourages the others on his team to do the same.

As a leader, he realizes that it is his responsibility to be aware of whether there is a balance between the recognition received by both the customer-facing and support positions within his organization. This balance can mean that he provides more on-the-spot awards for behind-the-scenes work or that he encourages others to give awards for the assistance they receive.

Maggio came up with an innovative idea so that all could celebrate the recognition that the team receives. Whenever anyone on the team receives a note of appreciation, whether in an e-mail or through an on-the-spot award, he puts a check mark on the "Thanks" board. When the team accumulates ten checks, they all go out to lunch. It is a popular program that reinforces the role they all play in getting those written notes of appreciation.

Through all his efforts, Maggio does an excellent job of demonstrating that recognition is important. He uses the programs provided, recognizes the need to closely monitor both performance and recognition, and supplements the programs with additional recognition that suits his team.

Great leaders take responsibility for people's enthusiasm for participating in recognition. Programs must be led. When there is commitment from the leadership, it says, "This is important. Make it work."

Company Values and Your Recognition Programs

Keeping the organization's values in front of employees is among a leader's many responsibilities. Leaders who regularly state the organizational values, mission, and strategic plan, and then demonstrate through their actions that they believe in these things, send a powerful, congruent message to employees. One of the best ways to reinforce that message is with recognition. John Mitchell, VP of Engineering at Pella Windows & Doors, believes in this philosophy. He sees value in Pella's recognition programs, such as Moment of Truth and Successful Teamwork Achieving Results (STAR), both employee-nominated awards.

Mitchell's approach to recognition isn't warm and fuzzy. He isn't focused on making employees feel good, and he rarely thinks about recognition as an end in itself. When asked about a traveling trophy award that he instituted, he said, "It grew more out of a desire to reinforce or recognize innovation than 'how do I reward employees?'" Mitchell's goal was to produce results.

Engineering already held a quarterly meeting where teams reported on how they were doing. Mitchell decided that it was the perfect forum to reinforce the importance of innovation. Now, each quarter, he asks the teams to prepare a presentation describing their most innovative idea of that quarter. As the teams make their presentations, senior management rates each idea. Before the

meeting ends, the scores are tallied, and the trophy, a twelve-inch
version of a Pella window, is presented to the winning team. They
get to display the trophy until the next meeting.

The contest itself and the recognition that comes from receiving the trophy put the focus on innovation. Mitchell says, "People think the Innovative Idea Contest is a lot of fun. Even though
many of the ideas will never see the light of day, it creates a lot of
energy and spurs further idea generation."

Part of leadership is defining and reinforcing mission, values,
and strategic plans. But leaders can't just tell people what is important and expect it to stick. They need to find ways to reinforce what
is valued. Recognition can do that. Think about what you would
like to emphasize: customer service, teamwork, or innovation.
Develop a simple program and take leadership. You will get results.

You are the leader of all recognition efforts. You need to
champion programs, giving them credibility and visibility. You
need to personally offer effective recognition, modeling it for
everyone within your organization. By your words and actions,
you will have a profound impact on recognition and, in turn, on
the success of your organization.

TAKING ACTION

- Focus on creating inherent workplace recognition. Demonstrate that you respect and value employees and the contributions they make.
- Get to know as many employees as possible. Talk to them
  frequently. Your interest in people's personal and professional
  lives is real recognition.
- Model good recognition habits. Others will follow your lead.
- Cheer the recognition efforts of others. Take the lead on any
  programs your organization rolls out. It's up to you to generate excitement and commitment.

chapter 6

Partnering with Program Administrators

Imagine you work for a company where the Human Resources department arranges for every employee to receive a potted plant on the anniversary of his or her hire date. The computer generates a list of employees with upcoming anniversaries, an HR employee creates the purchase order, and a florist delivers your plant. When your manager walks by your desk and notices that you have received the standard anniversary plant, she says, "Oh, is it your anniversary?" At that moment, how recognized do you feel? Does it matter to you that the people in HR know it's your anniversary? Unless you have a relationship with HR, it probably doesn't.

For most people, this kind of recognition has about as much value as a computer-generated birthday greeting from their life insurance company.

This isn't just a hypothetical example. This is the story of a real employee who was the victim of outsourced recognition. As her story illustrates, recognition only has meaning when it comes from people who benefit from your behavior or have a direct interest in your achievements. Recognition that comes from recognition program administrators, whether in HR or Communications, is cold, impersonal, and a waste of company resources.

To turn around the anniversary plant idea, the manager needs to play an active role. If your organization has a service program, participate. In this example, HR can still generate the anniversary list and order the plants, but their representative should deliver the plant and the name of the employee directly to you, the manager. HR might take it a step further and provide an anniversary card. After that, it's up to you to prepare a personal note and deliver the plant.

You will determine whether the anniversary gift
makes a positive impression, because it's the
interaction between the employee and manager,
and not the gift itself, that is meaningful.

A major reason recognition programs fail is that recognition gets outsourced to administrators. Remember the 50/30/20 Rule of Recognition. Employees want the majority of recognition to come from the manager. It is okay for administrators to support your recognition efforts, but not to provide the recognition itself. Here is another way to think about the administrator's role versus your role as manager.

The Administrator's Supporting Role

Every spring the Academy of Motion Picture Arts and Sciences gives out the awards known as the Oscars. Other than Best Picture, the awards that create the most excitement and get the most media attention are Best Actor and Best Actress. The actors and actresses nominated for these awards are Hollywood's stars, but the academy knows these people can't do it alone. They also give out awards for director, sound, special effects, editing, and more. The people who receive these awards are highly respected professionals with vitally important roles in the process of creating great movies. Without their support, films would never get made, and the stars would never shine.

Employee recognition also has starring and supporting roles, and, as with the Oscars, both types of roles are vitally important. Because the relationships people have with each other determine whether recognition works, the stars of employee recognition are the people being recognized and the people whose businesses, lives, and jobs they affect. A manager recognizes a team that has accomplished its objective. An employee recognizes his or her supervisor for providing needed support. A vice president recognizes a division for meeting a goal. Managers, supervisors, teams, and individual employees—these people are the stars of recognition that works.

In the best organizations, you, as a manager or supervisor, are responsible for recognition while your recognition administrator guides and supports you, remaining behind the scenes, influencing and coaching rather than trying to lead.

> The Ministry of Environment in British Columbia provides a good example of this approach. When the deputy minister wanted to focus on employee recognition, he asked Patricia Marsh, Manager of Corporate Safety, to take the lead. She chose to approach the project as a consultant-coach, communicating regularly with managers about the value of recognition, what great recognition looks like, and providing ideas on how managers can best recognize employees. The approach has been very effective, and they have been able to raise satisfaction scores significantly.
>
> Wells Fargo has an equally effective approach. According to Cheryl Miller, Recognition Manager for Wells

Fargo Technology Group, recognition coordinators (RCs) in her group work with managers to keep recognition efforts front and center. These RCs offer many services: they coordinate events, administer nominations, offer training and coaching, and much more.

Managers and supervisors at Wells Fargo can best leverage their RCs' support by doing the following:

- Include them in staff meetings to offer updates on recognition.
- Ask them to volunteer to lead a "fun committee."
- Have them compile nomination information from business partners and customers.

You may not have a recognition coordinator in your organization, but your HR or Communications team can probably provide you with some of the services described in the two examples given.

Wells Fargo RCs also provide managers and supervisors with questionnaires to help them learn more about what their team members want. They have graciously allowed me to reprint their questionnaire here for your use.

Their Good Intentions

When the people in HR discover that job satisfaction is suffering because employees crave recognition, they often find themselves in a frustrating position. They have identified a need and want to do something to correct the problem. If managers ignore the problem or plead that they don't have the time, often HR will take the lead. They create sophisticated and imaginative programs, survey employees on preferences, create metrics, and track results. While HR's intentions are admirable, inevitably, if you the manager don't drive recognition, their efforts are usually wasted.

Know Your Team

Use this form to guide an individual discussion with a team member and as a gathering spot for information you learn through casual conversation over time. Jot down ideas for little ways you can personalize recognition in ways you know will surprise and delight them.

Team Member's Name:

Corporate Hire Date (month/day):

Birthday, if they would like it celebrated:

Answers & Recognition Ideas
_____

Family:

Pets:

Interests/Hobbies/Activities:

What holidays do you celebrate?
Favorite restaurants:
Favorite beverage/food/snacks/candy:
Favorite way to relax:
Favorite way to "spoil" yourself:
Favorite vacation destination:
Favorite stores:
Favorite types of music/movies:
Favorite cartoons/characters:
Least favorite duty at work:
_____

How do you prefer to be recognized?
☐ Privately ONLY   ☐ Publicly and privately

Tell me a few favorite memories of being recognized.

Describe your ideal working environment.

What self-development events/courses would you like to participate in?

What can I personally do to make your job easier?

*As a manager who wants your people to feel recognized, you
have to be willing to accept responsibility for recognition.*

You can allow HR to support you but not replace you.

The Supporting Role in Action

HR can play an active and vital role in the recognition
process:

- Design and implement great programs.
- Track what works and what doesn't and use this
  knowledge to recommend effective changes.
- Train managers on the organization's recognition
  programs.
- Provide coaching to managers and supervisors.

An Example for HR
In the first edition, I featured FedEx Freight's HR as an example of what HR can do particularly around tracking and mon-
itoring programs. Because this edition focuses on what the
manager needs to know to be successful in working with HR,
this material is now available online. To learn more about the
tracking process, visit www.maketheirday.com/fedex.pdf.

Leveraging HR's Work

As you can see, HR can provide services that play a pivotal role
in the recognition process. The expertise this department provides is often crucial. HR staff can greatly assist your recognition
efforts. They can significantly improve the recognition process
and employee job satisfaction. You can leverage the work they do
in creating and managing programs, surveying, and offering
training to make you most effective. The Taking Action section
will provide some specific ideas on how you can have your recognition administrators help you with recognition.

*HR is there to support you, but it can't
offer meaningful recognition for you.*

TAKING ACTION

- Let your administrators know that you are interested in using recognition programs. If your organization has any programs, they will most likely be thrilled to show you what is available, include you in pilot projects, and ask your opinion of programs under consideration.
- Ask for an evaluation of your efforts. Many organizations survey employees, run focus groups, or offer multirater feedback tools that can help you improve. Ask what is available, and use the information HR gathers.
- Request training or coaching on how to provide meaningful recognition. Lots of resources for improvement are available. Your recognition program administrators can help you find the right fit.
- Get ideas. Your administrators can help you supplement existing programs with other complementary and creative recognition ideas. They may have resources in terms of awards, cards, and so forth, that they can attain for you. Ask and you will find that many HR folks are overflowing with ideas that you can use!
- Leverage existing programs. Program administrators make your job easier by handling the logistics of more complicated recognition programs. Take ownership of the programs they develop, and make them successful within your department. If you do, you will add variety to the kinds of recognition you offer employees.
- Be a program advocate. You can help create buy-in among your peers. Share your enthusiasm and success stories.

chapter 7

Making Recognition the Responsibility of Every Employee

What One Person Can Do

In the days before online ticketing, I called a travel agent to book an airline ticket. From the moment the agent answered the phone, I knew getting that ticket wasn't going to be easy. He practically spat into the phone, "Hello, may I help *you?!*" I thought about hanging up, but masochist that I can sometimes be, I persisted. Things only got worse. Within a couple of minutes, I was nowhere closer to getting my ticket and was frustrated enough to consider asking for the supervisor (I can do "indignant" really well when I want to). Instead, I decided to take the recognition approach and really *see* this guy.

"It sounds like you are having a really tough day," I said. There was total silence at the other end of the line, and I thought for sure that he had quietly hung up on me.

After what seemed like an eternity, he said, "I am. Two of my coworkers called in sick, and my boss is sending me all of their clients. I have twenty tickets to book for my own clients. I don't know how I will get it all done."

The whole interaction took less than a minute. The amazing thing was the change it made in his attitude and mine and, as a result, in the productivity of the interaction. To top it off, that energizing moment made me more positive and productive for the rest of the day. I imagine it had a similar effect on the agent.

By simply seeing the person behind the transaction, by valuing the individual, I was able to make a difference. This is recognition in the purest sense.

Taking the Initiative

In working with hundreds of burned-out and bored employees, I've found most share two beliefs:

- They believe their work environment is causing them to lose enthusiasm for their work.
- They believe they have no control over that environment.

In explaining their burnout, they describe bad bosses, uncooperative and/or lazy coworkers, rigid rules, and lack of communication. When I ask about recognition, inevitably they tell me that they don't get any. They tell me about managers and coworkers who are unappreciative of what they do.

When I ask if they *give* any recognition, they look at me like I have grown a second nose in the middle of my forehead; after all, we are talking about *their* burnout. The point they are missing is that people who get recognition are much more likely to give it, that working in an environment where recognition is common predisposes people toward offering it themselves.

If you are part of an indifferent, recognition-free environment, you might feel reluctant to be the first person to offer
recognition. This is understandable. When you offer recognition,
you acknowledge that other people contribute to your success.
You have to be willing to share the credit for your accomplishments; and when you're barely receiving any recognition, it is difficult to share. Do it anyway. Ultimately, the recognition you
offer others will improve your work environment and increase
the quantity and quality of recognition you receive in return.

Simple things make a difference, like writing a thank-you
note to a coworker who covered for you when you had to leave
early, or sending an e-mail to your boss telling him how much
you appreciated the way he handled a problem you brought to
his attention. If you want a more motivating work environment
with greater levels of appreciation, take the initiative. Offer
recognition to your boss, coworkers, and the people you lead.
You will see an increase in the amount of appreciation everyone
receives. You will improve your own job satisfaction and the satisfaction of everyone around you.

Understanding Peer Recognition

Peer recognition can be very powerful. It's easy to see how a workplace where employees show each other appreciation would be a
more pleasant place to work. Employees who recognize each other
show greater respect and tend to act more cooperatively. Respect
and cooperation create a happier, more productive workplace—an
obvious benefit for individuals and their managers.

Peer recognition can take three basic forms. It can be very
unstructured and spontaneous, with employees simply acknowledging each other as they choose. It can be loosely structured,
with the organization providing the awards and some criteria but
letting employees decide when and how to give them. It can also

be more formally structured, with systems in place for selecting recipients and managing the entire process.

Manager's Time Tip

Another benefit of creating a culture with plenty of peer recognition is that it increases the overall frequency of recognition. In a department with twenty employees, a conscientious manager may offer significant recognition to each employee once every other week. If employees in that department are in the habit of recognizing each other and each employee recognizes just four coworkers each month, the amount of recognition the average employee receives would nearly triple, significantly upping the chances that each employee would feel adequately recognized. This approach increases recognition without increasing the manager's workload.

Wells Fargo Bank's Internet Services Group, the division that handles all online banking, offers a good example of an organization that uses a variety of peer recognition options.

According to Jean Bourne, Senior Vice President of Human Resources, a survey of the Internet Services Group's fifteen hundred employees, completed in 2001, revealed that only 50 percent of the employees were satisfied with the recognition they received. When her department spoke with managers to see what could be done, their response was "We are just moving so fast, we sometimes don't take the time to recognize everyone's contributions." Her team wanted to make it easy for everyone to provide recognition without significantly increasing anyone's workload, so they designed the E-wards program.

Online Recognition Program—
Wells Fargo's Internet Services Group

- **E-cards.** These are simple online thank-you cards. Anyone can give them to anyone else, anytime. The online site guides givers through the process, asking questions and providing examples of how they might use the cards. The givers can copy the manager if they choose. Another copy goes to a special recognition mailbox where cards are collected for a quarterly drawing for prizes.
- **E-wards.** These nominations praise consistent performance over time. Anyone can complete an online form nominating anyone else. Categories are listed, and nomination examples are available. Managers must approve a nomination, returning it to the person making the nomination for further clarification, if needed. Rarely is a nomination denied. After approval, the winner's manager gets three things: a certificate that details the nomination, a scratch-off ticket that will reveal a $50 to $200 prize when it is scratched by the winner, and a sheet that provides ideas on how to present the award, depending on the recipient's preferences.
- **Ride the Wave.** To create even more excitement for the first two programs, once a year all e-card and e-ward recipients are eligible for inclusion in a special event. A committee of senior managers reviews the cards and nominations and selects seventy exemplary employees to attend a three-day off-site event with a guest of their choice. The event combines professional development with fun and a lot more recognition.

In 2001, Wells Fargo's Internet Services Group employees sent sixteen hundred e-cards and more than nine hundred e-wards—with continued growth in 2002. Employees seemed to love the program. However, a follow-up survey didn't show the improvement that Bourne's group expected. The next step was to run focus groups to get to the source of the problem. Feedback showed that the programs are great. People loved the peer recognition. At the same time they said that peer recognition didn't replace the need for other forms of recognition. Many still wanted more direct recognition from their managers. They wanted their managers to use the program. They also wanted them to offer public praise, group recognition, and a simple "Thanks—I appreciate your hard work." This is another example of the 50/30/20 Rule in action.

Informal Peer Recognition

When you begin to acknowledge the people you work with, you have begun your own informal peer recognition program. You may be doing nothing more than thanking someone who assisted you on a project or sending an e-mail to someone's boss to describe how that employee helped you.

Sandra Clark, a University of California–Santa Cruz employee, told me about the drawer of kids' tools she has; it contains toy screwdrivers, hammers, and more. When someone in another department helps her "fix" something, anything from her computer to a personnel problem, she sends a tool and a "fix-it" award thanking them for their help. It's not an organization-wide initiative; it's her way of showing appreciation. It's a simple courtesy that requires nothing of management and, over time, can positively affect the atmosphere of her workplace.

Peer recognition can be completely unstructured and left to the discretion of employees. Managers and their organizations can also take a slightly more organized approach to informal peer recognition, like Wells Fargo's Internet Services Group did with the e-card (not e-ward) program. Typically, when you, the manager, is involved in informal peer recognition, you need only provide the awards or prizes, some ideas about when they should be awarded, and a little encouragement. The rest is up to employees.

Informal Peer Recognition Ideas

You might use some kind of card or certificate that allows the giver to fill in the recipient's name and describe what that person did that was noteworthy. I have seen these called many things:

- Star Bucks
- Caught in the Act Notes
- Brag Certificates
- Thanks a Bunch Cards

Regardless of what they are called, these cards offer a medium for thanks or praise. Usually, recipients can also redeem them at a later date for gifts or entry into some kind of a raffle.

Don Peden, a manager at LSI Logic, a semiconductor company, helped his HR department through a difficult time by encouraging his people to develop their own informal recognition program. After a massive reduction in workforce that had taxed their department's resources, they held a debrief session. In that session, Peden provided thank-you notes so that people could take a moment to show appreciation to anyone who had helped them through the process. Those notes ended up posted on bulletin boards and cubicle walls for several weeks afterward. By providing the supplies and a few minutes to write notes, Peden made it easier for employees to show their appreciation.

> ## Values-Based Recognition Idea
>
> Provide "Values Medallions." Print one value on each medallion. Employees give the medallions to those people who help them in some way and demonstrate a company's value. The giver of the medallion also provides the recipient with a very specific description of why that person has received the medallion, reinforcing the valued behavior. The medallions should have a Velcro tab or some other way employees can display them on their cubicles. (Idea courtesy of Xilinx)

Nominations

Many companies use formal peer-nominated recognition systems. Done well, peer nomination can be a very effective recognition strategy. You saw one example with Wells Fargo's Internet Services Group's e-ward program; Pella Windows & Doors does something similar.

> Employees recommend each other for "Moment of Truth Awards." The basis of Pella's Moment of Truth philosophy is the assumption that every decision and action by employees affects product value and the satisfaction customers receive. When employees see a coworker doing something above and beyond what is required, they submit that person's name for a Moment of Truth Award. Managers review the recommendations; as with Wells Fargo's Internet Services Group, most of the time they

approve the award. The reward is small but highly valued—a Moment of Truth pen presented by the employee's manager and VP in front of their peers. Monthly recipients of the award are then mentioned in their internal publication.

When Great Plains Software became the division of Microsoft called Microsoft Business Solutions, it brought with it another excellent example of how effective a structured peer-nominated recognition program can be. At Pioneer Days, the company's annual awards ceremony, they gave out twelve different peer-nominated awards. Awards included the Sodbuster Award for overcoming obstacles, the Harvest Award for quality, the Jesse James Award for innovation, and the Eagle Award for leadership. As so often happens after an acquisition, this program has been replaced. It is still worth referencing for the clear example it provides.

Anyone who sees another person living the
company values can nominate that person.

Managers were actively involved in the Microsoft Business Solutions program. This wasn't a program designed to allow managers to pass off responsibility for recognition. Anyone could nominate anyone else. Managers nominated their own employees as well as employees from other departments. Employees nominated their managers as well as their peers. It was perfectly acceptable for a stock clerk to nominate the president and vice versa.

Pioneer Days offered recognition that works because employees knew what it took to win each award. Nomination letters were read during the presentation, providing a clear explanation of why a particular person received the award. The letters helped keep the

What did Microsoft Business Solutions employees think of the awards and what they represented?

"It was really rewarding to know that my peers thought I made a great contribution. The camaraderie and the congratulations that I received from fellow team members after the awards ceremony was extremely fulfilling."
—Chris Lerum, Manager, Tools and Technology Support

"I have always felt that by my receiving recognition for breaking the rules and asking hard questions, it has become okay for other folks to do so as well."—Matt Gustafson, Program Manager

"Every time I attend Pioneer Day Awards and watch people I have met or worked with receive awards, listening to the great things they accomplish, and seeing some of their work personally, it always inspires me to do more and become better at what I do."—Angela Hoy, Team Manager

"The great thing about the tradition of recognition at Great Plains is that it is consistent, fair, and diverse. People are recognized from all over the company for all kinds of good works, and I get to work with these people every day."
—Karl Gunderson, Software Design Engineer

"It was very rewarding to know that I made a difference, that my customers appreciated the services I provided to them. It motivated me to work even harder to provide the best customer service I can."—JDee Muir, Print Service Specialist

program from becoming a popularity contest. They also reinforced the culture and values of the company by allowing employees to see examples of what is outstanding. For details on this program, go to www.maketheirday.com/microsoftbusiness.pdf.

Taking Responsibility

Wells Fargo and Microsoft offer two examples of formal peer-nominated recognition programs. Many companies have these types of programs. If your company has a nomination program, use it frequently. Write detailed nominations with specifics of what you value and how the nominee embodies those values.

As a manager, you should take the lead on using the peer recognition program. Just because it is called peer recognition it doesn't usually mean it can't be used with direct reports. In fact, managers and supervisors have found that when they use these programs, not only are employees thrilled by the manager recognition, but they also are more likely to use the program themselves. Increased usage means more recognition overall.

What if your employer provides no structure for peer recognition or you simply want to supplement the organizational recognition offered?

You may be wondering what you can do on your own, without organizational support. Let's look at this from the perspective of the manager and then from that of the individual.

What a Manager Can Do

You can start your own peer program. Keep it simple. Cards with tear-off stubs that are submitted for drawings or a traveling trophy are two good possibilities. You might also look at creating a recognition committee within your group or department that can create new programs.

The IT group of the British Columbia Lottery Corporation did exactly that. As a result of a manager meeting, they formed a recognition committee. Their goals:

- Promote recognition across all levels.
- Make recognition easy.
- Complement HR's programs.

Four years later the committee is still going strong. They organize two big events every year. A few years ago they created a "RecognITion Wall" where notes of congratulations and appreciation are expressed by managers and peers alike, and where IT department milestones are recorded on brick plaques and added to the wall in bricklaying ceremonies. They developed recognition books for peer recognition that travel from recipient to recipient. The result of their enthusiasm? IT has the highest engagement and lowest attrition rate in the company.

Don't want to create a program? You don't have to. Here are a couple of ideas that take little organization:

- Give a gift card as a spot award. When you present the card ask, "Who helped you be successful?" Give the recipient enough gift cards that she can reward these people herself.
- Implement FASTER meetings (see the box on the next page). These provide an opportunity for employees to show praise and appreciation in a frequent, structured, and relaxed manner.

What an Individual Can Do

Everyone can find simple ways to acknowledge the efforts of the people you work with. Offer your appreciation in a thank-you

FASTER Meetings

FASTER meetings provide everyone with a turn to talk, yet as the name implies, they are *fast!* They are so fast that many teams hold them standing up.

Here is how they work:

- Hold frequent meetings; daily or weekly is most common.
- Give everyone one minute to talk.
- Have each team member address the following:

Finished: What has he completed since the last meeting?
Acknowledgments: Who made his job easier? (Praise and Appreciation)
Still outstanding: What is he working on now?
Trouble spots: What difficulties is he encountering?
Enlightenment: What has he learned?
Requests: What does he need?

The FASTER meeting provides a status update, allows the lead to reallocate tasks, gives opportunities for self- and peer recognition, and builds understanding of the responsibilities of others. Give it a try!

card, or praise your colleagues' work to their supervisors. Employees have told me that their coworkers' thoughtful gestures have made their day. Try bringing back small souvenirs from your vacation, offer congratulations to someone receiving a degree, and give a vote of confidence to someone who is promoted.

With just a bit of creativity, you might also design and implement your own simple peer recognition program, just as the university employee did with the kids' tools.

If the type of recognition described on the following pages seems silly to you or, more important, would seem silly to the people you want to recognize, stick with a simple thank-you or praise for a job well done. Give a card, send an e-mail, or tell them in person. After all, it's like your mother always said: "It's the thought that counts."

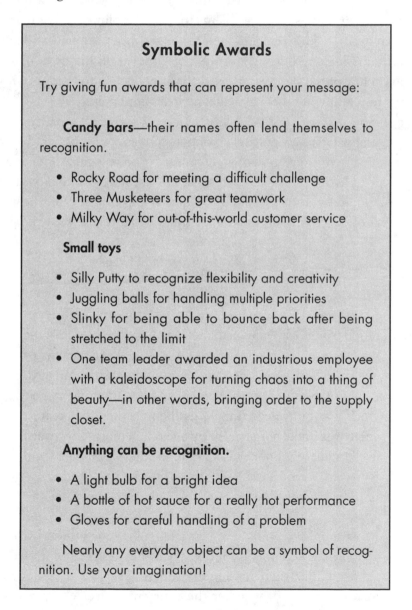

Symbolic Awards

Try giving fun awards that can represent your message:

Candy bars—their names often lend themselves to recognition.

- Rocky Road for meeting a difficult challenge
- Three Musketeers for great teamwork
- Milky Way for out-of-this-world customer service

Small toys

- Silly Putty to recognize flexibility and creativity
- Juggling balls for handling multiple priorities
- Slinky for being able to bounce back after being stretched to the limit
- One team leader awarded an industrious employee with a kaleidoscope for turning chaos into a thing of beauty—in other words, bringing order to the supply closet.

Anything can be recognition.

- A light bulb for a bright idea
- A bottle of hot sauce for a really hot performance
- Gloves for careful handling of a problem

Nearly any everyday object can be a symbol of recognition. Use your imagination!

Recognizing Up

While you're at it, don't forget to recognize your own manager or supervisor. Few people ever think to recognize up. Ask employees whom they recognize at work, and if they mention anyone, it would be subordinates and peers. Managers are the people employees bring problems to, not compliments. For many employees, acknowledging their manager in a positive way feels like "kissing up," "brownnosing," or "apple polishing," to name just a few of the slang terms used to show disdain for people who try to manipulate their managers with compliments.

How do you avoid being labeled a brownnoser? It is pretty simple, really. First, recognize everyone, regardless of his or her ability to influence the direction of your career. If you recognize both your peers and your manager, your peers are less likely to think you're being manipulative. Second, don't be manipulative. Be sincere. Don't offer recognition to get something. Do it to give something.

Managers appreciate recognition as
much as the next person.

Many managers have told me stories of meaningful recognition from their team members. Michelle Boyes, one of the managers mentioned in Chapter 4, shared that a member of her team had nominated the team for a national award. Boyes felt honored that a member of the team thought their work was of award-winning caliber. For her, the greatest value was in the nomination by a team member. The award itself, while an honor, was less significant. When their team won the award, Boyes used the cash prize for a team celebration, bringing the recognition back full circle.

Most employees take good management for granted when they have it and complain loudly when they don't. If employees would recognize their managers and supervisors in a sincere manner, regardless of whether they currently receive any recognition from them, they would see a positive response. Just because some managers rarely give recognition doesn't mean they don't value it. More likely, either they feel underappreciated themselves, or offering recognition simply hasn't occurred to them. In either case, employees who recognize their manager's efforts and accomplishments are more likely to receive recognition themselves.

A Simple and Effective Tool

Peer recognition works whether it is highly structured like the Microsoft Business Solutions program or completely under individual control like the university employee's fix-it awards. Peer recognition improves employee relationships and the frequency of recognition.

Appreciation and acknowledgment spread from person to person and can change an entire organization. To develop a culture where peer recognition is the norm, the change can begin anywhere. With a little effort, anyone can have a significant impact on his or her own department. Shift supervisor, filing clerk, technician, or team leader—regardless of where peer recognition begins, it can make a big impact and dramatically change the atmosphere of the workplace, resulting in higher productivity.

TAKING ACTION

- Create an environment where people are encouraged to recognize their peers, both on and outside your team.
- Implement FASTER meetings.
- Model good recognition habits.
- Recognize anyone who has a positive impact, not just those on your team.

chapter **8**

Using Self-Recognition to Improve Quality

Taking the Initiative

There is one company where the employees don't wait for someone else to make their day. They recognize themselves. They create scrapbooks filled with their accomplishments, along with photos, certificates, and letters from their customers. They prepare presentations to tell their coworkers about the dozens of improvements their team has made to operations. They take employees, managers, and the executive team on a hard-hat tour of a catwalk to show off a safety improvement they've made. Employees in this company take the initiative when it comes to recognizing themselves for the improvements they make.

What drives these employees to recognize themselves? Are they desperate for recognition? No. As a matter of fact, an internal job satisfaction survey at this company showed 81 percent overall employee satisfaction with the recognition. Employees recognize themselves because their company values and promotes self-recognition.

Desperate for Recognition?

Scenario: You are on a team that has completed a successful project, and you'd like to get the accomplishment recognized around the office. How can you do this without coming off as a braggart?

Collecting Those Kudos

- Publicly congratulate your coworkers for their individual accomplishments. Be sure to point out any accomplishments that might be a little off the manager's radar.
- When you talk about your accomplishments, emphasize how others helped you even if it was by taking up the slack while you got the project done.
- Describe what you learned from the experience. This turns the conversation into a development discussion rather than an opportunity to brag.
- Compliment your boss once in a while. Make it genuine. Do it privately. Managers are often the most underrecognized group out there. They are operating at a recognition deficit. Give them a little praise, show them a little appreciation, and they may recognize you and everyone else a little more frequently.

How Do You Know You've Gone Too Far?

Share the wealth using the methods listed, and you aren't likely to go too far. Just in case, watch for reactions which you recognize. Do people look bored, frustrated, or annoyed? You might have stepped over the line a bit. You will know you're having the right effect if people want to work with you, acknowledge you, and respond to your requests quicker.

Graniterock is a privately held, one-hundred-year-old company of about eight hundred employees. Its biggest recognition event is an opportunity for self-recognition. Its turnover rate is one-fifth of the industry average, 90 percent of its employees say it is a great place to work, and 88 percent plan to stay until they retire. Graniterock is clearly not a company that treats its employees poorly.

> Graniterock employees get recognition. It takes many forms, from full-page ads thanking them for volunteering for community service to breakfast with the president and CEO Bruce Woolpert on their first day of work. Keith Severson, Marketing Services Manager, shared with me that when he had "Breakfast with Bruce," he sat next to another new employee, a cement-mixer truck driver. This driver told Severson that, in fifteen years on the job, he had never even met the president of his previous company. He was amazed to find that on his first day he was having breakfast with the president of Graniterock. This driver felt like an important part of the company. By simply having breakfast with these new hires and showing that he is accessible, Woolpert recognizes the value of the people Graniterock hires. He offers recognition that works.

Leaders, managers, and coworkers at Graniterock do a good job of recognizing people. So why are they so proud of the recognition that they give themselves? The executive team believes that every employee is an entrepreneur, a leader within the organization. They don't refer to employees as employees, but as Graniterock People, and Graniterock People are expected to find problems and correct them. It is everyone's job to constantly improve the company and make sure that they receive acknowledgment for those improvements. Everyone is responsible for his or her own recognition. In fact, they have an obligation to share their accomplishments with their coworkers, and Graniterock has devised a program that helps them do this.

Celebrating Recognition Days

The greatest opportunity for self-recognition at any Graniterock facility is Recognition Day. Recognition Day always has an enthusiastic audience. Employees see their facility's Recognition Day as "their time," their opportunity to strut their stuff, not just in terms of their accomplishments but also in terms of their creativity in putting together the event. Employees plan the event, choosing the theme and location. Groups have held their events on-site in order to show off recent innovations. They have also held them in more nontraditional locations. It is up to the volunteers who plan the event. To demonstrate safety improvements for working at night, they held one Recognition Day on the side of the freeway at 3:30 in the morning. Another was held at a shopping mall before it opened one morning, and two others were held at a miniature golf course and bowling alley where every hole or lane had a different presentation complete with review questions and prizes. Groups take advantage of the unique environment of each location in order to create excitement and reinforce the ideas they are presenting.

The presentations themselves are even more diverse than the locations employees select. People are free to use their own creativity to decide how they want to make their presentation. They make scrapbooks and posters, offer tours and demonstrations. It's their choice. They also choose what accomplishments to recognize, highlighting the achievements they most value.

Although this event might seem best suited for white-collar workers who are comfortable making public presentations, at Graniterock everyone gets involved. Ricki Mancebo, a truck driver, discovered a three-way mirror that allows drivers to see better. She checked out the practicality of having one installed on every truck and then oversaw the installation. For Recognition Day, she gave a demonstration of the increased visibility the mirror provided, using her truck as a visual aid.

A branch manager, Carl Jaco, who began nearly twenty years ago as a driver, remembers his first presentation. He, too, had made improvements to his truck. He chose to assemble a book on those improvements, complete with pictures. He gave his presentation, made it through his nervousness, and became excited about self-recognition and Recognition Days. It made such an impression on him that he says he still has the book he created.

There is a lot of energy and excitement around Recognition Days. Even so, some new hires show a little reluctance to participate. Their managers try to get them to attend at least one Recognition Day before they make their own presentation. Usually that is all it takes to hook them on the idea. People see Recognition Day not only as an opportunity to show off their accomplishments but also as a chance to get to know each other and share ideas while they learn and continue to improve.

Using Individual Development Plans

Many organizations have individual development plans (IDPs). When creating a development plan, individuals work with their managers to set goals for growth and improvement for the coming year. Finally, they select activities and learning opportunities that will help them achieve those goals.

On the surface, an IDP may not appear to be recognition at all, but when you remember that opportunity is one of the four elements of recognition, you will see the role an IDP can play.

Graniterock's development plans (referred to as IPDPs) use self-study, coaching, and cross-training for many learning opportunities. Management has found that these methods

Manager Takeaways

What can you learn from Graniterock's Recognition Days?

- **Self-recognition doesn't replace other types of recognition.** Instead, it is a very effective supplement.
- **Some people will be hesitant at first.** They may be shy or afraid that others will think they are showing off. Let them observe before presenting, provide presentation coaching, and allow presentations that don't require public speaking.
- **Success is contagious.** As employees observe the accomplishments of their coworkers, they will think of new ways to improve. They will create new challenges and new successes to self-recognize.

What can you do to make self-recognition part of your team's culture?

- **Make self-recognition acceptable.** While you might not implement recognition days, you can certainly implement the FASTER meetings described in the previous chapter. The structure acknowledges that self-recognition is not only acceptable but expected.
- **Ask employees to train others.** They can show off their knowledge, and others will benefit by learning something new. One software company instituted "Bug of the Month," and no, they weren't recognizing the biggest disaster. They were highlighting the most intriguing solution. What a great way to increase learning and recognition at the same time!

are inexpensive and very effective. They favor cross-training, in particular, because of its ability to improve organizational focus, teamwork, knowledge, and skills. These learning opportunities will work for you as well.

Chances are good that your organization has a structure for development plans. Don't worry if you don't have anything formalized. Either way, you will find some tips here that you can use with your team.

Creating a Simple Development Plan

Even without a formal structure, you can help employees plan their development. Work with them to answer these three questions:

- **List the major responsibilities that are essential to your job, and put a star by those made possible by last year's development.** In this section, employees list their primary responsibilities. You can use this section to coach employees on those responsibilities that are most valuable to the company.
- **Describe what you want to learn during the next twelve months.** The employee creates a list of developmental objectives. That list can include increasing product knowledge; improving customer service and safety; and understanding the company objectives, policies, and procedures. Work to develop a list that seems beneficial to both the company and the employee.
- **List the corresponding experiences/activities and observable measures that will meet these development objectives.** Here you answer the question of how the employee is going to meet his or her objectives. Work with your employee to set short- and long-term goals for training and development. List observable measures for new skills learned.

Here is one example of some related learning objectives: meet three key customers, cross-train with another employee, devote a number of hours to self-study, and attend an off-site customer service workshop. Notice that not all learning opportunities involve formal classroom training.

Tips from Graniterock on Using Development Plans

- **Make as many senior-level managers as possible aware of the development plans of each employee.** This visibility improves employee career options. When employees see multiple opportunities for growth within their organization, they are more likely to stay with the organization and remain enthusiastic.
- **Don't treat the development plan as a performance review, and don't make it a requirement.** Employees should see the development plan as an opportunity to learn and grow. Use it to recognize their value to the organization.
- **Be creative in selecting learning opportunities.** Don't limit your options to formal training. Consider mentoring, self-directed learning, and cross-training. Learning opportunities are everywhere.
- **Work with employees to create and implement the plan.** Give them as much control as possible while helping them improve their value to the company.

Adding Self-Recognition to the Mix

Self-recognition is a powerful and underutilized form of recognition. Few managers ask employees to recognize themselves. If you aren't encouraging self-recognition, you are missing an excellent opportunity. By adding self-recognition to your existing recognition mix, you can encourage employees to showcase their most important accomplishments. When employees control their own recognition, they receive validation for what is most meaningful to them. After all, who knows what an individual wants more than that individual? Self-recognition allows you a glimpse into what employees value so they can use that information to create other forms of recognition that will be meaningful. Finally, self-recognition adds to the frequency of recognition. It increases the possibility that every employee will feel sufficiently recognized.

TAKING ACTION

- Encourage employees in your department to acknowledge their accomplishments. Make self-recognition acceptable. Spend a few minutes in your weekly meeting asking employees to recount a success from the previous week.
- Plan for success. Work with employees to set development goals. Encourage them to explore a variety of learning opportunities. Review and celebrate their progress and help them recognize their own potential.
- Convince employees that they have an obligation to share their successes because everyone benefits when they do. The answer to how one person overcame a particular challenge might provide the answer to someone else's pressing issue.
- Make self-recognition fun. Celebrate. Get employees excited about participating. The quality of recognition will go up, and you will have an excellent learning experience for everyone involved.
- Acknowledge your successes. Most of us are in the habit of ignoring the good that we do and focusing on our mistakes. Keep a journal of your accomplishments. Refer back to it when you need a boost.

PART 3

Making Recognition Work

chapter 9

Getting Specific and Relevant

Lesson from a Fortune Cookie

Crack open a fortune cookie, and you get a fortune that's nearly always true. Yet you will rarely find the message interesting. Why? Because it is vague. In the writer's attempt to make the fortune relevant to everyone, it becomes relevant to no one. You can learn a recognition lesson from the fortune cookie.

Vague recognition that could apply to anyone
doesn't leave people feeling recognized.

The Employee of the Month Award is the classic example. Typically, there are no set criteria for receiving the award. It's simply given to an employee identified as doing a good job. Without set criteria, Employee of the Month leaves workers asking questions: "How is this month's winner a better employee than I am?" "Am I doing a good job?" "What exactly do you have to do to become Employee of the Month?" If employees can't find satisfactory answers to these questions, the title quickly becomes meaningless. People won't strive to win the award if they don't know what it takes to win it. If, by chance, they do win, their sense of pride will be limited because they won't know what the award represents.

When you play a game, you want to know
the rules before you begin.

Think of the last time you played a game: a sport, board game, computer or video game—anything that you like to play for fun. Did you know the rules of the game before you began? Did everyone play by the rules? What would happen if you all played by different rules or someone cheated? Your first reaction might be frustration. You might attempt to get everyone to play fairly by the same rules, but if that failed, you would probably lose interest and quit. The same thing is true with recognition. When recognition is ineffective, frequently it is because no one knows the rules of the recognition "game."

Playing by the rules means you judge and recognize performance based on preestablished criteria. This increases the likelihood that your recognition will be perceived as fair. It builds trust when you play by the rules, and employees who work in an atmosphere of trust are happier and more willing to work cooperatively.

So, how do you establish the rules of recognition? You begin by identifying the values, goals, and behaviors that lead to success.

What Do Values Have to Do with Recognition?

The Microsoft Business Solutions peer recognition program discussed in Chapter 7 was based on the group's mission and shared values that were integral to their culture. The program reinforces their organizational culture because it allows employees the opportunity to see examples of what is outstanding.

Ask a Microsoft Business Solutions employee why a coworker won the Heritage Award, and that person would know. When the award was presented and the nomination read, everyone learned why the nominee was chosen to receive the award. They knew the nominee's actions embodied the values that they all shared. Ask a recipient if the award had meaning, and you would get a resounding yes.

Values Help Avoid Unintended Results

Recognition that isn't based on strongly held organizational values gets limited results, no results, or the wrong results. Setting goals, particularly goals accompanied by financial incentives, without creating a strong foundation in values is potentially dangerous. Consider the following example:

> For a chemical manufacturer, a top concern should be safety. Its people should live and breathe safety. If everything they do isn't focused around promoting safety, then a goal to reduce the number of accidents reported would only lead to a reduction in the number of accidents *reported*, not necessarily a reduction in the number of accidents occurring. This is especially true if recognition is accompanied by a financial incentive.

Even if the manufacturer puts a high value on safety, some employees would still find it tempting not to report minor accidents if it meant they would get a bonus. To reduce the possibility of this happening, management needs to confirm that they recognize and reward only desired behaviors. They need to ask themselves the following questions:

- Do we emphasize the importance of *being* sa
  appearing safe?
- Do we value consistency in following safety
  than having speed and profit our primary cor
- Do we recognize and reward ideas that will imp
  rather than proving everything is perfect the way it is?
- Do we recognize and reward people for reporting and correcting violations rather than overlooking and concealing violations?

Your goals and actions have to clearly support the company's key values. In the chemical manufacturer's case, the key value is safety. If you were a manager in this organization, you would want to reinforce safety in everything you do, from communicating project strategy to the recognition you offer. There should be no doubt about your priorities.

You don't have to be a manager to communicate and reinforce values. Wherever you are within your organization, the values you hold and communicate should align with the organization's values.

Remember, you are defining the rules of the game.

Clarifying values helps define the objective. It begins to answer the questions "What do we have to do to win?" and "How do we know when we have won?" The answers determine how employees will behave.

Values Provide Purpose and Meaning

Have you ever heard employees say, "What's the point?" They may be burned out and need serious guidance or coaching to get them back on track. Or it may simply be that they don't understand how their work fits into the bigger picture. An understanding of their value to the team and/or organization motivates most people.

Can the people who work with you describe what your organization, division, or department values? Do they understand your business model, your mission statement? If not, you need to communicate that information.

Know what you value. Know where your organization going, clarify your departmental or team goals as the the bigger goals, and know how you plan to get nicate your strategy clearly and frequently. Provi with the necessary resources. Work these things int your organization or department. Then use recogniti force what is important.

> Recognition as a tool to reinforce values and goals can be extremely effective. I learned this lesson firsthand while consulting for Raytek Corporation, an international company that manufactures infrared thermometers. Years ago, when Raytek first became my client, I was touring the company's offices and noticed something intriguing. Everywhere I looked, people's cubicles had plastic apples on display. When I asked about them, I learned that the apple awards were given, along with an extra vacation day, to employees who used no sick time during the previous year. As my guide continued to explain, I learned that the company placed a high value on saving money. Much of their corporate culture was based around that value. The people at Raytek were proud of their ability to improve profitability by reducing costs, and management acknowledged their efforts. One way employees helped save money was by using sick time only when they were sick, rather than using the time as discretionary personal days. The days off were a valued reward, but the apples were a lasting symbol of their contribution. Employees were proud of what the apples represented.

Linking Goals to Individual Performance

Peak performers want to do work that matters. For their 1999 book *First, Break All the Rules*,[1] Marcus Buckingham and Curt Coffman of the Gallup Organization sifted through more than a million interviews to determine what matters most to top performers. They found twelve workplace characteristics most critical to these employees. These characteristics are frequently referred to as the Q12. According to the research, one of the twelve characteristics concerns whether the "mission/purpose of my company makes me feel my job is important."

Employees are more willing to take the initiative when they understand the mission, values, strategic plan, and goals of the organization. Being able to see how these relate to individual performance is motivating. Part of your job, in recognizing individuals, is to establish a clear link between the organization's values and goals and the individual's goals and behaviors. The link between these two is shared goals.

Shared Goals and Performance

Effective organizations set high-level performance goals. Each level in an organization then sets goals that align with all the entities they report to. The goals of a business unit may only need to align with those of the organization, while the goals of a cross-functional team might need to align with the goals of the organization, their division, and each of their individual departments.

To illustrate this point, take a look at how the various departments of a large nonprofit agency might align themselves with a company-wide goal to reduce costs.

- Employees in Client Services look for more cost-effective ways to serve their clients.

- Volunteer Education chooses to implement an online learning solution to reduce the expense associated with traveling around the country to provide training.
- Marketing employees test the response rates of a direct mail campaign using postcards instead of letters. They know that if response rates are comparable, it will mean a significant savings on postage.

At each level, groups pursue separate goals, but their goals all align with the cost-cutting goal of the organization.

So, how are shared goals developed?

Shared goals can be developed by management and dictated to employees, but you will find it more effective to use a collaborative process. Let employees help set shared goals, and they will have a better understanding and greater ownership of those goals. They will also be more likely to achieve them.

Setting collaborative goals together provides the group with a strong sense of clarity about what those goals mean. This improves employees' sense of purpose. To further emphasize that sense of purpose, recognize groups when they achieve a shared goal. You might celebrate the achievement of small goals with an announcement and doughnuts or pizza (employees and managers alike say that food is a requirement for any celebration!). For bigger goals, dinner for the group, along with a formal acknowledgment, might be appropriate. Regardless of the form it takes, when you recognize shared successes, you provide an opportunity for everyone in the group to be a winner.

Individual Goals and Performance

Group goals provide a framework for individual performance goals. Understanding what motivates the organization, division, department, or team helps employees align their own goals and gives them a greater sense of purpose.

Employees in the Volunteer Education department of our previously mentioned nonprofit share the organization-wide goal to reduce costs. They know that online training can be very cost-effective in some instances, so they choose, as their department goal, to implement an online learning solution to help educate the agency's volunteers.

Several members of the department set individual goals to become familiar with available learning technologies. Together they will select the most cost-effective solution. Other members choose to focus on which courses can best adapt to the online format and provide the most cost savings. Alex embraces his department's goal to implement online learning but chooses to balance the department's cost-saving efforts with his own efforts around another shared value—customer service. Volunteers are the customers of their department, so with his manager's guidance, Alex chooses to survey volunteers to determine what they want from training. He is excited about the project because he is clear that his contribution will make the online learning solution better.

When the survey is complete, Alex has successfully captured the volunteer perspective; he knows what they want. Alex's manager asks him to act as the implementation team expert on that perspective. While Alex is the obvious choice for this role, the new responsibility is also a form of recognition. It recognizes the value of Alex's contribution to the team.

Help employees select goals that align with your shared values and goals. Clarify tasks and roles so that each person can recognize his or her own unique contribution. Help employees discover, understand, and even extend the magnitude of their contribution,

Reinforce Your Values

A team leader wanted a novel way to recognize the people on her team during a retreat. I gave her the following assignments to help her prepare:

Assignment 1: Make a list of everyone on your team. Next to each name write at least one behavior, skill, or attitude that this person brings to the group. She told me that this exercise gave her a greater appreciation of those on her team. "Frankly," she said, "there are a couple of people I hadn't realized brought anything to the team!"

Assignment 2: For each individual, think of (and purchase) an inexpensive object that symbolizes one of their positive attributes. This process takes a bit of imagination. She found having someone to brainstorm with really helped.

Assignment 3: Prepare a presentation where you will talk about the positive attributes of each person, present the gift, and make the connection between the object and what you just said. This team leader gave each person a creative and meaningful award. For example, she gave a rubber chicken to the guy who brought his sense of humor to a stressful work environment and a toy telephone to the woman who always maintained her professionalism when talking to upset clients.

Starting with a list of what she valued about each person, she was able to create an event that communicated those values and reinforced individual performance beautifully. It was an event that few are likely to forget anytime soon.

and you help them recognize the value of their own achievements. In turn, they will be more enthusiastic and productive.

Recognize individuals who achieve their goals using the approaches discussed earlier in this book. With smaller goals, you will probably want to offer recognition one-to-one. A private verbal acknowledgment or a handwritten or e-mailed note is appropriate. If the goal was a significant milestone, announce it in a team meeting or provide a gift certificate when you acknowledge the achievement, whatever is most appropriate for the individual.

High-Performance Behaviors

Employees like recognition that is specific, relevant, and *frequent*. According to the Gallup survey (*First, Break All the Rules*) mentioned earlier in this chapter, peak performers want to be recognized at least every seven days. This presents a challenge. If you help each employee set and achieve about ten goals for the year and recognize the employee for every achievement, recognition is still too infrequent.

You probably couldn't handle the workload that would accompany setting fifty-two goals per employee per year. There are two solutions for the frequency problem that are more manageable and effective. The first solution is to get everyone involved in the process of recognition: team leaders, coworkers, even the individual him- or herself. Look back to Part 2 of this book for ideas on how to do this. Second—and the point I want to address here—is that you want to recognize behaviors as well as goals. Together these two things will expand the opportunities for recognition exponentially without overburdening you, the manager.

Problem: Many goals take months, even years, to accomplish, and recognition needs to be frequent to be effective.

Solution: Recognize both *accomplishments* and the *behaviors* that lead to those accomplishments.

Specific Recognition Makes Their Day

Recognized behaviors, like goals, need to be specific. When people tell you they appreciate that you offer several possible solutions when you present a problem, you know exactly what they value. You can't say the same thing when they compliment you on your positive attitude. Do they mean they like that you don't mention potential problems? Do they like that you tell jokes in the break room every morning? Or do they mean that it's great that you let them push you around without complaint? With vague recognition, their meaning is left up to the imagination.

Vague: Positive attitude
Specific: Treats customers and coworkers with respect.
Tackles projects outside the scope of the responsibilities of the job.
Rarely complains, prefers to look for solutions.
Brings a bit of fun or humor to every meeting.
Treats failure as a learning opportunity.

Clear, specific recognition of behaviors is meaningful. It provides guidance, strengthening the working relationship with the person giving the recognition. Compare the impact of these two thank-you notes:

> Jan,
>   Thank you for your work on the new accounts receivable system. Your efforts are appreciated.
>   Thank you, Sara

While many employees would be thrilled to receive this much recognition from a manager or coworker, consider how much more meaningful it would be to receive the next version.

> Jan,
>
> Just a quick note to let you know how much I appreciate the initiative you've taken with our new accounts receivable system. I understand some of the processes are less than intuitive and that many members of the implementation team are already frustrated. Your efforts to understand the quirks of the system and assist your team members in overcoming them will help us to achieve our goal of a flawless transition and help us to serve our customers better when the new system is in place.
>
> Thank you, Sara

It takes more time and effort to be specific, and people appreciate that effort. Send a thank-you note like the one in the second example, and you tell the recipient she is important because you know precisely what she did that was commendable, and you took the time to tell her. Send a thank-you note like the second example, and you offer recognition that positively impacts performance.

> The mother of a young Staples office supply employee told me, "[At Staples] they have 'I noticed' cards. There is no value attached. It's just a note from the manager saying what she noticed the employee doing. My son has every one he's received posted on a board at home!"

Specific recognition tells employees exactly what they are doing that is valued. On each of the Staples' employee's "I noticed" cards, his manager had communicated what behavior she considered commendable and told the employee that he exhibited that behavior. This young employee responded to being "noticed."

Remember the fortune cookie. Vague, unspecific recognition that could apply to anyone leaves employees feeling unrecognized. Specific, detailed recognition, based on your organizational goals and values, is most meaningful. Communicate "the rules"—the specific goals, desired behaviors, and intended purpose of recognition. Use recognition to emphasize the group and individual efforts and results. Work to provide fair, specific, and frequent recognition, and you'll provide recognition with meaning.

TAKING ACTION

- Offer specific, meaningful recognition by telling employees exactly what they did and why you value their behavior or contribution.
- Evaluate your recognition efforts by asking yourself these questions:
  - ☐ Is my recognition focused on the most important issues?
  - ☐ Have I clarified how recognized behaviors and outcomes support what I value?
  - ☐ Am I confident I'm recognizing the intended behaviors and outcomes and not others?
  - ☐ Have I achieved the results I anticipated?

Measuring for Results

Why Measure?

Sports teams keep score. They also track averages, handicaps, assists, and receptions. Anything that measures performance gets reported. Statistics give players objective feedback. When a player receives the award for most valuable player, good statistics usually back it up. Those statistics help make the award fair and consistent from year to year. Measurement makes the award relevant to both players and spectators. In your organization, you measure for the same reasons—to track performance. When you measure and then use that information in your recognition, you provide objective feedback and make the award relevant to recipients and observers alike.

Getting Results

A Toastmasters International club in Amherst, New York,[1] provides a good example of measurement in action. Clubs and associations have always had difficulty getting members to take on leadership roles. Lacking the ability to offer financial rewards, volunteer organizations have to rely on other ways to motivate members. This Toastmasters club in Amherst previously had a great deal of difficulty getting people to volunteer long enough to gain the experience needed to take on the role of president. Members would serve as treasurer or VP of education and then step down. Few members felt ready or willing to take on the responsibilities of president.

The club needed to find a way to get members to rotate through all the officer positions, gain experience, and then step into the president's role as the culminating activity. The question that faced the group was "How do we get members to step up to the challenge?" They found an answer. They started measuring and recognizing participation and got results!

WHAT THEY VALUE:	Volunteers for leadership positions
THEIR GOAL:	To have members hold every leadership position
WHAT THEY MEASURE:	Which leadership positions members have held
THE RECOGNITION:	The title of Terrific Toastmaster

After a member has served six months in every leadership role, that person's name is engraved on a plaque and his or her contribution highlighted in the club newsletter.

It sounds simple—and it is—but the results are still impressive. Members who had previously been reluctant now challenge themselves to become Terrific Toastmasters, and the pool of potential presidents has increased significantly.

What to Measure?

Last year, Suzanne Danis-Harkness, Manager of Application Maintenance and Support at Home Hardware, began documenting her measurable results. She updates this report monthly and says, "It feels good to see what I have accomplished and to meet with my manager on a monthly basis and review the results." Her manager was pleased with the process, so together they decided to expand its use within the department. Danis-Harkness is now using it with her direct reports to measure accuracy, spot a need to rework code, and determine whether they are up-to-date and meeting estimates.

To decide what to measure for your direct reports, start, as Danis-Harkness did, by finding appropriate measures for yourself. Once you are proficient in this area, you can develop measures for your direct reports.

You may be thinking, "Our work isn't measurable. The work I supervise is different." The truth is that most jobs can be measured for specific results. Look at your values, business strategies, and goals before you decide what to measure. They can provide focus. Measures should provide tangible proof that you are achieving your goals within the boundaries of your values.

As mentioned in the previous chapter, you can usually achieve your goals by more than one method. With a strong incentive, people will achieve success in ways you never considered. As you'll see in the following example, some of their methods can produce undesired results:

To reduce costs, one strategy used by some HMOs is to measure the number of referrals doctors make to specialists and base bonuses on that measurement. The fewer referrals doctors make, the bigger their bonus. If the HMO holds two key values: profits and the health and well-being of their patients, its objective might be to limit only unnecessary referrals. The problem is the only value it is measuring and rewarding for is profit.

Most doctors will choose to continue to stress patient health on their own, but some will get caught up in the measures and rewards. These doctors will produce fewer referrals, reasonable or not, increasing HMO profitability and their own bonuses. But at the same time, they will jeopardize patient health.

Although such a scenario is less likely with recognition than it is with an incentive such as a bonus, it is still true that you are more likely to achieve what you reinforce. To achieve the HMO's goal of reducing unnecessary referrals, it will need to find a way to also measure a doctor's commitment to patient health and well-being.

Carefully tie measures to your existing values and goals.

Verify that what you are measuring only measures the desired result.

Look for relationships among your values, goals, and measures. The following example will help you strengthen connections between them and recognition.

Let's look at an example of a measurable goal that is tied to values. Your goal is to reduce annual turnover, the percentage of the workforce that leaves each year. If the current turnover rate for your group is 32 percent a year, and you are expected to reduce that by one-third to 22 percent, reducing turnover to 22 percent a year becomes the measurable goal.

Note the relationship that exists between the three values and the corresponding measurable goal. High job satisfaction results in reduced turnover, and reduced turnover typically results in increased productivity and profitability. If you focus on reducing

VALUES	MEASURE	MEASURABLE GOAL
High job satisfaction Productivity Profitability	Employee turnover	Reduce turnover from 32 to 22 percent annually

turnover by increasing job satisfaction, you should see improvement in productivity and profitability as well. The following example shows how you might use recognition to support this goal:

> Challenge employees to help reduce turnover. Emphasize the impact that everyone has in creating a positive work environment. Have employees create departmental values and related goals to help them achieve the turnover goal. When they succeed in reducing turnover by one-third, have a celebration to announce their success.

Taking Stock of Current Measures

Assess your current methods of measurement. Note what you measure and how your measures relate to your values and goals. Use this information to clarify your recognition objectives and generate recognition ideas based on measurable criteria.

Consider getting help in selecting appropriate measures. Administrative groups within your organization can be terrific resources, as noted in Chapter 6. They may already track much of the information you need and can help you define new measures. Finance already tracks profits, revenue, and costs. Human Resources probably tracks sick days taken, turnover and employee satisfaction rates, safety records, and the percent of employees mentored or trained. Lots of information should already be readily available throughout the organization. Consider statistics such as productivity, defect rates, follow-through on qualified leads, rate of repeat business, number and nature of complaints, and customer satisfaction ratings.

Collecting Data

In this section, you will learn to select data sources and make appropriate use of the information you gather. When considering the validity of any information you use, hold it up to the following criteria:

- Measurements should provide quantifiable data.
- Measurements should be consistent over time.
- Measurements should create an accurate picture of current conditions.

Let's look at each one in more detail.

Make sure you can quantify the information you gather. For example, how do you measure for job satisfaction? Is it enough to observe that employees seem happier? No, it isn't. Measuring takes a vague concept and makes it tangible. You can find numbers that relate to job satisfaction. As already mentioned, turnover rate is one good indicator. Number of sick days taken can be another. You can find many more. Whichever indicators you choose, make sure they are measurable.

Be consistent over time. Use the same measurement for an extended period. This approach will help you identify trends in your data.

Use measurement to create an accurate picture of current conditions. The big question to ask yourself is "Am I really measuring what I think I am measuring?" If additional training can improve job satisfaction, does that mean the number of training days taken is a good indicator of job satisfaction? It might be, but if people are required to complete training they think is worthless, job satisfaction may actually go down. To avoid misinterpreting data and making erroneous assumptions, use multiple measures from a variety of sources. For instance, using the number of days trained, current turnover rate, and results of a job satisfaction survey would provide a more balanced picture.

Quantitative Resources for Measuring Success

Review of Financial and Operational Documents
As mentioned earlier, your organization already tracks data. Balance sheets, income statements, financial ratios, and production, service, and regulatory reports all provide excellent quantifiable (measurable) information. Most of this information has already been compiled, using the same methodology, for long periods of time. It's a free source of data that should help you identify trends. See what's already available before you choose new methods of data collection.

Questionnaires and Surveys
Questionnaires and surveys can be great for gathering opinions. They can provide inexpensive, consistent, and quantifiable data that offer a candid, accurate picture—but only if people believe you will keep their responses confidential, and only if you can elicit enough responses to make your survey representative. Also beware of the following concerns in choosing to do a survey:

- Surveys can be viewed as impersonal, especially with smaller groups.
- Poorly designed questions can influence participant responses and skew the results. Use caution in designing your own sur-

veys. You can use the two surveys in the appendix at the back of the book in their entirety or as a guideline.

- People will have an expectation of change. If you ask employees if they are satisfied with manager recognition, they will expect you to address any deficiency.

Qualitative Resources for Deeper Analysis

One-on-One Interviews

If you have a small group, you can use one-on-one interviews to gather both quantitative and qualitative information.

With larger groups, one-on-one interviews are best used to dig deeper into survey results. One-on-one interviews can help you discover *why* respondents answered the way they did. This additional information, though not measurable, is valuable because it helps clarify survey results, allowing you to learn more about the issues the survey reveals.

Consider the following potential problems when using one-on-one interviews:

- Because of the lack of anonymity, you will get less candid responses if interviewees are uncomfortable with the interviewer.
- Interviewers with a bias toward a specific outcome can skew results by leading respondents toward their preferred response.

Focus Groups

With a focus group, a skilled facilitator provides the topic and guides the group through a discussion. Some of the advantages and disadvantages are similar to those found in one-on-one interviews. Like one-on-one interviews, focus groups provide an excellent opportunity to explore unanticipated issues and clarify survey results. They are also better for gathering qualitative rather than quantitative information. And like the negative impact an interviewer can have in a one-on-one interview, a focus group can be adversely affected by choosing the wrong facilitator.

Focus groups also have their own unique advantages and disadvantages. For example, being part of a group can stimulate participants to talk about issues that they might not have considered in a one-on-one interview. At the same time, if participants of the focus group know each other, they may not be willing to openly discuss the topic being explored.

Observation

Observation isn't usually appropriate as a measurement tool, but it is valuable for recognizing behaviors. Providing recognition that works requires that you gather data by observation and then use that information to correct or recognize the behaviors that affect performance. You might observe whether employees are friendly to customers, keep the production area clean, or offer suggestions for improvement. Observation is also the basis of most employee-nominated awards. It is appropriate for this purpose so long as the awards recognize clearly articulated behaviors.

Data Collection Recap

Choose your data sources carefully. Determine what is appropriate in each situation. Have multiple measures, and use those measures in your recognition efforts. Remember, measurement helps make recognition more meaningful. Just as sports fans appreciate statistics on their favorite teams and players, employees like "knowing the score." Measure workplace performance, and you provide an objective yardstick that will help you create meaningful and memorable recognition.

TAKING ACTION

- Provide recognition based on the data you collect.
- Measure your ability to meet your goals using quantifiable, time-tested data.
- Collect information from a variety of sources.
- Look to existing resources for measurement data before developing new data sources.
- Use qualitative data to support quantitative data.
- Ground your measures in values to help counter the success-by-any-means mind-set.

chapter 11

Aligning Recognition with Culture

When I step through the front lobby, the first cubicles I approach are brightly decorated with awards, photos, mascots, and the trappings of the latest contest. These are the desks of the customer service team. Heading deeper into the building, I notice a distinct change in atmosphere. The tone is much more somber. I am now in the section of the building where the engineers work. As their surroundings show, the personalities that are attracted to these two jobs appear to be very different. With just a few steps, I have experienced two distinct microcultures within the same organization.

The customer service team in this example would call the engineers' recognition preferences boring. The engineers would say that the customer service team holds silly contests and embarrassing events. Both would be right. As different as these two groups are, both have *exactly the right recognition for their culture.*

People want awards that their peers would admire.

Part of the recognition experience is receiving recognition that not only you personally prefer but that your peers will also admire. This means getting recognition that is a fit for your culture.

Doing a Culture Check

Your team has a culture. That culture is formed by the team's personalities, generations, nationalities, work styles, as well as by your industry. It is even affected by whether everyone works in the same location.

It is important that you recognize the culture of your team and take it into consideration as you plan your recognition activities. To help you better understand your team's culture, let's look at some of the factors that influence it. As we explore influencers, it can be very easy to fall into stereotypes. Remember, these guidelines are only a starting point to getting to know the preferences of your team.

Culture/Recognition Mismatches

Here are a few of the mismatches I have come across in my work:

- Construction workers—happy face pins
- Traveling salespeople—gift certificate for dinner out
- Recent Asian immigrants—Employee of the Month picture in lobby

In each case, the award illustrated to employees that the organization didn't understand its own culture. The recognition sent or reinforced the message that people weren't valued.

Considering Industry and Job Preferences

Patterns to employee recognition preferences are directly related to the kind of work people do. Some personalities are attracted to certain jobs, and these personalities seem to share some likes and dislikes.

Here are a few examples:

- Construction workers, truck drivers, scientists, and engineers generally don't want "silly" recognition.
- Those in jobs with high levels of customer interaction tend to be more open to a playful approach.
- Salespeople and customer service reps often respond well to contests.

If you have spent significant time in your industry or have even held some of the positions you are now supervising, you can probably trust that your overall preferences are similar to your team's preferences. If you are an outsider (or just feel like one), don't assume that the recognition, awards, and celebrations you prefer will satisfy your team.

Identifying Generational Preferences

Have you heard?

- Young workers just don't have the same work ethic as past generations.
- They won't listen to authority.
- And they don't have the same pride in their work as other (i.e., older) employees do.

Sound familiar? In fact, I have found similar statements written about Millennials, Gen X, *and* Baby Boomers. With each generation, we seem to puzzle about the work styles, work ethic, and preferences of our newest workers. So, if you've found yourself wondering, "What do they want?" you aren't alone.

In 2008, I surveyed over eight hundred people regarding their preferences, age group, and years in the workforce.[1] This research uncovered three key factors:

- The variation in preferences is less than might be expected.
- Variations do exist and are worth considering.
- Even the least valued recognition and rewards have their fans.

Let's look at each of these separately.

The variation is less than might be expected. Between age groups, the differences in preferences are not all that dramatic. All age groups have the following in common:

- They appreciate receiving time off as an award (the number one choice).
- They like gift cards as spot awards (the number two choice).
- They want meaningful, interesting, and challenging work.
- They need clear expectations and understanding of their role to be most engaged.
- They love praise and appreciation.
- They need some kind of social interaction.

There are no categories of recognition that one age group loves while another disdains.

Variations do exist and are worth considering. For all the similarities, there still are differences, and while subtle, your attention to these differences can make you a hero with your employees. The following box shows the top preferences for each age group.

What Interests Those 56+?

Work environment:

- They prefer interesting work with minimal supervision.
- They expect their manager to ask for and respect their opinions.

Spot awards:

- Time off was the first choice for 60 percent.
- Gift cards or certificates were the first choice for 27 percent.

What Interests Those 46–55?

Work environment:

- They have overall high expectations for the work—interesting, challenging work that uses their strengths and talents, with opportunities to grow and develop.
- They also have overall high expectations for work communications.

Spot awards:

- Time off was the first choice for 55 percent.
- Gift cards or certificates were the first choice for 32 percent.

What Interests Those 36–45?

Work environment:

- They also have overall high expectations for the work—interesting, challenging work that uses their strengths and talents.

- They enjoy anything that contributes to doing meaningful work.

Spot awards:

- Time off was the first choice for 53 percent.
- Gift cards or certificates were the first choice for 41 percent.

What Interests Those 26–35?

Work environment:

- They enjoy interesting and meaningful work.
- They want to be provided with clear expectations.
- They like frequent feedback and encouragement.

Spot awards:

- Time off was the first choice for 61 percent.
- Gift cards or certificates were the first choice for 27 percent.

What Interests Those 25 and Under?

Work environment:

- They want opportunities to learn, grow, and develop.
- They like adequate guidance on not just what to do but how to do it.
- They enjoy frequent social opportunities for interacting with coworkers and supervisors.
- They like lots of positive reinforcement.
- They prefer a clear separation of work and personal time.

Spot awards:

- Time off was the first choice for 56 percent.
- Gift cards or certificates were the first choice for 35 percent.

Even the least valued rewards have their fans. The final point that this survey illustrates is that within each age group are exceptions. A trophy or plaque was least valued overall, but a small percentage of people listed this option as most valued.

Regardless of the age group, every option had its fans.

Dealing with a Dispersed Workforce

Years ago, when I first noticed the trend in people working from locations apart from their supervisors, I interviewed managers and one of the questions I asked was "What would allow you to comfortably supervise people working from home?" One manager responded, "Video cameras." He wanted to be sure they were working!

Hopefully, your management style doesn't require your intimidating presence in order for work to get done. Still, managing people who rarely see you or their coworkers does present some challenges. Not the least of these is recognition.

If you recall that recognition is about *seeing* and *acknowledging* people, the challenge becomes obvious. As the supervisor of a virtual team, you are responsible for both recognizing people and encouraging them to recognize each other. This is no easy accomplishment when people are in different parts of the country or world.

How do you provide an environment where people feel valued when they are physically located in more than one place? Keep the following in mind:

• The need for clear expectations and goals is as strong as and even stronger than when you are in the same location as employees. Use a results-based work model.

> **A dispersed workforce poses the following issues:**
>
> - Limited face time
> - Different time zones
> - Lack of familiarity and trust
> - Significant differences in other cultural factors

- Good communication processes are even more critical. When someone falls out of the loop, he or she feels invisible.
- Respect is still the key. Take time zones into consideration when planning meetings and checking in.

Using Technology to Assist You

Technology has made it possible for virtual teams to exist. It can also help you create great relationships between you and your team. Try the following:

- **Use your videoconferencing system.** It is good for frequent one-on-ones. The telephone will work as well, but the face-to-face contact docs help. These video one-on-ones will effectively supplement your occasional live meetings.

  You can even use your conferencing system for team building. I worked with one manager who used the company's system for Friday afternoon movies. Each location rented the same "B" movie and cued them up at the same time. They turned on their conference rooms' videoconferencing systems and laughed and joked together as they watched the movie.

- **Create a recognition area on your intranet.** Provide a space for your team where they can post photos and a profile. Add any

letters of congratulations you receive onto a virtual bulletin
board. Note team and individual accomplishments. Encourage team members to leave comments as well.

- **Use collaboration software.** Use it not only for project management but as a place to leave positive comments on the work
as it commences.

Remember, these few ideas are just a beginning. Technology
changes quickly and can provide you with new ways to bring
people together.

One final thought on working virtually: Don't let technology
become a crutch. Although technology is a terrific help in maintaining contact and visibility, it can also be a barrier. Make time
for meeting in person whenever possible.

Changes in Global Team Recognition

In today's work world, it is highly likely that you are working
with teams comprised of people in or from more than one country. Perhaps your company is multinational, or you may have
recent immigrants on your team. Either way, it is important to
understand the preferences of those from different parts of the
world.

As you can see in the Mercer study highlighted in this section,
there are some significant differences in what drives engagement.
It is important to note these differences in terms of both what and
how you recognize.

Mercer's findings fit quite closely with my observations in
working with teams in a number of these countries. I especially
want to draw your attention to the results from China. Common
wisdom is that those from Asian cultures don't like individual
recognition. While it is true that being singled out in front of the
group can be embarrassing (e.g., the Employee of the Month

Engagement Factors around the World

According to a Mercer study,[2] recognition is a driver of engagement in all twenty-two countries surveyed. Here are the top factors in several countries, according to their findings and as they relate to recognition as defined in Chapter 1:

- Australia: quality of workplace relationships, including coaching
- Canada: being treated respectfully; good work/life balance; feeling they can provide good service to the clients or customers
- China: sense of personal accomplishment; good reputation for customer service; training opportunities; regular performance feedback
- India: type of work; promotion opportunities
- United Kingdom: sense of personal accomplishment; training opportunities; good reputation for customer service
- United States: confidence that career objectives can be met; sense of personal accomplishment; confidence in organization's success; quality as a high priority; opportunity for growth and development; information and assistance to manage career; flexibility to provide good customer service

photos mentioned earlier as a culture/recognition mismatch), that doesn't mean that Chinese employees only want team recognition. On the contrary, the survey findings from China indicate that a sense of personal accomplishment is the highest-rated item. If you supervise people in China or who are immigrants from China, focusing only on the team would be a mistake. Offer individual recognition—privately.

So, what about awards? Again, if you are working with people who live in different countries, it helps to understand the culture to select the best award. For instance, gift cards are very popular in North America and Europe. They haven't caught on in China, where a gift such as electronics or candy is preferred. In India, celebrations around local events are appreciated, as are forms of recognition that include family.

But as different as we all are, in some ways we are very much the same. My research shows that time off is the most desired spot award around the globe.

Your team may be very diverse in age, location, and the kind of work that they do. They might all be very similar. Either way, understand the culture of your team, and select recognition that is most appropriate.

TAKING ACTION

- Identify the cultural influences that affect your team.
- Show a genuine interest in learning about their countries of origin.
- Have an open discussion about the challenges of working in remote locations.
- Brainstorm together to find appropriate solutions.

chapter 12

One Size *Doesn't* Fit All

Personalizing Individual Recognition

Picture the following scenario. Alli is responsible for producing the specifications for her team's latest project. Maritza, another member of her team, volunteers to stay late one evening to help Alli finish those specifications. Maritza didn't have to do that, so to show her appreciation, Alli gives her a Mars candy bar. She tells her it's for "out of this world" teamwork. Alli gives a candy bar to everyone whose assistance she considers noteworthy. It's a clever idea that emphasizes Alli's point—that Maritza's contribution was exceptional. It's a gesture that Alli hopes will strengthen their working relationship. The problem is, Maritza is a diabetic. Alli's choice of a recognition symbol, a candy bar, shows Maritza that while her contributions matter, her personal needs don't. Instead of strengthening their relationship, it may damage it.

Employees subjected to mass recognition, with no appreciation of their unique needs and interests, feel only half-acknowledged. To be most effective, you need to acknowledge both the achievement and the person behind the achievement. This is true of all recognition, but it's especially important with individual recognition. You can't always consider everyone's unique concerns when you offer group recognition, but there is no excuse for impersonal individual recognition.

Some people will argue that individual recognition is counterproductive. They say it creates jealousy and resentment, and that the only way to promote teamwork is to recognize the entire team. Team recognition is important. So is organization-wide and departmental recognition. They can create a sense of cohesiveness. But the importance of group recognition doesn't preclude the need for individual recognition.

A 2007 Make Their Day survey found that 82 percent of respondents believed the most meaningful recognition they had ever received had been given to them as individuals.

People want to know they're valued as individuals, particularly those employees who are most engaged and productive— the peak performers. Even if they consider themselves team players (and most do), high-achieving employees don't want all of the credit to go to the team.

An employee from IBM said his manager sends a handwritten note to each direct report on the anniversary of his or her hire date. The note recounts the employee's contributions for the year, describing how he or she is important to the department. People in his department look forward to receiving and sharing these notes with each other. The manager recognizes the unique contributions of his people. In return, they feel a sense of loyalty toward him.

Recognition is most meaningful when it takes into account the talents, skills, concerns, needs, affiliations, and accomplishments of the people you are recognizing. People want you to know something about them before you choose how to recognize them. They are especially impressed if the recognition is unique and especially selected for them.

> A maintenance officer in the air force received an award that he considered both unique and meaningful. The award was a hand-drawn picture of the three types of aircraft he maintained, mounted with photos of the eighteen people who worked with him in his section. He said this one-of-a-kind award was the most memorable recognition he had ever received.

The Issue of Fairness

When you individualize recognition, fairness does become an issue. People can confuse being treated the same with being treated fairly. It is important that you understand how to manage expectations and deliver recognition that is fair. It is so important, in fact, that the next chapter is completely devoted to the topic of fairness. For the time being, set your concerns aside and let's look at what you can do to provide individualized recognition.

The Process of Individualization

When you take time to listen and get to know an individual, what he or she values, and the quality of that person's work, you are offering a powerful form of recognition. Regardless of whether you are the employee's supervisor, someone from another department, the CEO, or a person they work with every day, personal attention gives recognition greater impact.

To better focus your attention and increase the positive impact, consider using this three-step process for individualizing recognition:

1. Identify how each individual contributes.
2. Determine personal recognition preferences.
3. Recognize unique contributions with personalized recognition.

The following sections will describe how to best accomplish each step.

Identifying the Contribution

> Assess productivity by asking workers what tasks they do, what they believe they should be contributing to the company, and what hampers them in getting the work done.
>
> —PETER DRUCKER[1]

If your work is affected by the contribution of someone else, you should be offering individualized recognition of specific accomplishments and behaviors. Regardless of your role in the organization, pay attention to how others contribute to your ability to accomplish your goals. Use that information to acknowledge how they have helped you. Step 1—identify how each individual contributes—helps you provide simple recognition that works.

The Manager's or Supervisor's Responsibility

If you're a manager or supervisor, there is a lot more you can do. Traditionally, it's your responsibility to help employees identify how they, as individuals, will contribute to the organization and then track their progress. Do it right, and the process itself is loaded with inherent recognition. Employees want to know they are making a contribution. They also want to know someone with the ability to influence the direction of their career is interested in their progress and wants to help them advance. When you show employees that you want them to succeed, they know they are valued. They feel recognized.

The Contribution Conversation

The easiest way to find out how employees can better contribute to the organization (and therefore improve their level of recognition) is to ask them. As the manager, you should schedule at least one meeting per year with each employee to discuss how that person's job contributes to the organization's values and goals. The purpose of this meeting isn't to assess performance, although that's certainly a related conversation. The purpose of this meeting is to develop a better understanding of how the employee views his or her job and to correct any misconceptions about the importance of his or her contribution.

To begin this conversation, explain the purpose of the interview and review the organization's values and goals. The following example shows how this discussion might progress:

> "Ray, I asked you here this afternoon to discuss how your role as salesperson helps us achieve our organization's goals and maintain our values. Just so we are clear, I am not questioning whether your contribution has value. I simply want to ensure you are doing work that you see as valuable.
>
> "As you know, XYZ Corporation has based its business model on four key values: profit, innovation, quality, and adaptability. The goals for the coming year are to

release one new product, upgrade three products based
on customer preference surveys, and find a new market
for two existing products."

This statement sets the stage for the questions that follow:

How do you see your work contributing? This question, or something similar, helps the employee explore his job responsibilities
and relate those responsibilities back to the values and goals of
the organization. Again, make sure the employee understands
that you are not questioning the value of his work but want to
discover how he *perceives* the value of his contribution.

> Ray responds that, as a salesperson, his sales contribute
> to the profitability of the company. Also, the company
> uses the information he gathers from customers to dis-
> cover consumer preferences. This information helps the
> company develop new products that will be in high
> demand.

**What tasks are you currently assigned that don't support these organi-
zational values and goals?** The purpose of this question is twofold:
(1) it helps streamline operations by uncovering redundant,
unnecessary responsibilities, and (2) it helps employees understand how their specific tasks contribute to the values and goals
of the organization.

> Ray thinks the time he spends compiling statistics on the
> number of lost sales is a waste of time, which may or may
> not be true. It's a point worth exploring and clarifying.

Can these tasks be modified to make them more relevant? This question explores, in greater depth, the employee's response to the
preceding question. You can encourage the employee to make
appropriate changes to how he or she performs a task so as to
contribute in a more meaningful way.

Ray's manager suggests that, along with the number of lost sales, Ray could track why the prospect didn't purchase their product. This information could be used to develop, upgrade, and expand their current markets.

What new responsibilities would allow you to contribute to an even greater extent? This question explores how an employee would make his or her contribution more relevant and valuable and helps the manager provide opportunities for growth.

Ray tells his manager he wants to work with Research and Development, facilitating a series of customer focus groups that explore customers' preferences in depth.

In this conversation, you see Ray and his manager clarify Ray's value to the organization. It provides Ray with the opportunity to recognize his own contribution, while the manager learns how Ray perceives that contribution. Ray learns something about how his responsibilities actually impact the organization. His manager helps him modify some of the tasks that he sees as a waste of time and shows him the value of others. Together they also explore new opportunities, discuss their feasibility, and identify appropriate action items that will make Ray's work more meaningful. The discussion and resulting changes show Ray that his manager is aware of his value to the organization and supports his desire to have an even more positive impact.

> *This contribution conversation can provide you and your employees with important information.*

You learn what they value and how they perceive the jobs they do. This information allows you to stay up-to-date on how employees already contribute and how they want to contribute in the future. Employees learn how their responsibilities affect their organization, which helps them make a more meaningful contribution. Because you, as the manager, are aware of their value, your employees feel recognized for both their current and potential contribution.

Determining Personal Preferences

Employees I spoke with across the country had diverse answers when asked about recognition that had lasting impact. As mentioned earlier, one said that being asked to take the president's place on a panel discussion was an honor she would never forget. Another valued his manager's willingness to have him work whenever and wherever he wanted, as long as the work was done. A third said having her direct supervisor praise her work to the department head was something she appreciated.

Ask ten people what type of recognition they most value,
and you will most likely get ten different answers.

Preferences vary with each individual. To see firsthand how different recognition preferences can be, copy the survey in this section, complete it yourself, and then ask friends and family members to do the same. You will see that your preferences and those of the people you survey vary significantly.

In my interviews, few people specifically said it was the personalization of the recognition they received that made it memorable. Even so, as they described memorable recognition, a pattern became clear: personalized recognition has more meaning. This makes sense when you consider that personalized recognition makes a positive statement about the quality of the relationship between giver and receiver.

One employee of a high-tech company was definite about what makes recognition high-impact for her. She told me her most memorable award was an overnight trip for her and her husband to a woodland resort area where they would be able to hike and spend time outdoors. It was memorable because, according to this employee, "it was tailored specifically to what I like to do." The fact that her supervisor knew her well enough to select that trip as a form of recognition was invaluable. The personalized recognition she received strengthened her relationship with, and sense of loyalty to, that supervisor.

Information about hobbies, job aspirations, friends, family, and even whether someone is gregarious or shy will help you discover what each person would appreciate. Regardless of your role in the organization, you show people that they are important to you, the team, and the organization when you select recognition based on their individual interests.

Remember, just knowing an individual's aspirations and interests is a form of recognition.

Everyone can personalize the recognition they give. Leaders can assemble special teams to research recognition options for milestone events. Teams can ask members to share what forms of recognition they prefer, using the information to recognize each other. Individuals can observe their coworkers and learn what hobbies and other outside interests they have, using that information to thank each other or acknowledge their contribution. Managers can apply any of these methods. They can also provide a more structured opportunity to discover their employees' preferences.

Managers and Supervisors Interview for Preference

If you are the manager or supervisor, you can use a preference interview to help you get to know employees better. The preference interview is nothing more than a structured conversation.

Which Do You Prefer?

Check all that apply:

- ☐ Time off in exchange for the extra hours worked to meet a project deadline
- ☐ A gift certificate for dinner for two as acknowledgment for a glowing letter of praise from a client
- ☐ A catered lunch for your department to celebrate an achievement
- ☐ The ability to determine your own hours, so long as the work gets done
- ☐ An opportunity to voice your opinion on critical issues
- ☐ Creative control over a project
- ☐ New responsibilities that you choose for yourself
- ☐ The chance to telecommute one day a week so long as you remain productive
- ☐ The opportunity to select your own professional development courses and seminars
- ☐ The opportunity to train other employees
- ☐ A story in the organization's newsletter about your valuable contribution
- ☐ A certificate of achievement
- ☐ An announcement of your accomplishment at a staff meeting
- ☐ The customer service champion (or top sales producer, etc.) parking place for the next month
- ☐ A sincere, handwritten note from your manager
- ☐ Other _____

_____

Like the contribution conversation, it can help you build recognition into the work, creating more job satisfaction. You may find some overlap with the discussion about employee contribution, but not necessarily.

Begin the preference conversation by clarifying your purpose. Let the employee know that you want to ask a few questions in order to better understand what would make her work more enjoyable. Once the employee is comfortable with the purpose and process of the interview, you can begin. Listed here are some open-ended questions about preferences, along with some possible responses and hints on how the information might be used to recognize and motivate.

What do you love about your job?

Response 1: "I love that I can leave at 5:00 most evenings to be with my family." To keep this person happy and productive, you shouldn't habitually ask her to stay late. Recognize and reward her with time off to be used at her discretion.

Response 2: "I love the independence that I have to do the job as I see fit." If the job is getting done satisfactorily, you will want to make sure this person remains unrestrained or unrestricted. This person will appreciate increased autonomy because it recognizes her ability to work independently.

Response 3: "I love solving a customer's problem and seeing the smile on his face when he leaves." Promoting this person to a position where interaction with other people is limited would probably damage her job satisfaction. It would be better to recognize her value by providing new opportunities to use her people skills and problem-solving abilities.

As your manager (or supervisor), what could I do to make your job more satisfying?

Response 1: "I would like you to help me prepare for a promotion." An excellent way to recognize this employee would be to introduce her to key managers or provide a coach or needed training. Many managers would hesitate to groom valued employees for a promotion because they don't want to lose them. But if you get a reputation as someone who helps people advance their careers, you will usually find that many desirable candidates are waiting to take the departing employee's place.

Response 2: "You could provide more social opportunities for the department." This employee values the social bonding of the group. You can recognize her by also recognizing the entire department with impromptu pizza parties and team-building activities at meetings. This employee would probably also appreciate being put in charge of birthday celebrations.

Response 3: "You could let others know how hard I work, so they don't try to dump their stuff on me." This employee wants public recognition for her contribution. Based on the emotion evident in the response, there might be more going on here. You would want to explore this response further.

How would you like to be recognized? It's better if you've learned the answer to this question during regular interactions with the employee, but if not, asking this question now will help you learn more about employee preferences. If the employee doesn't have any ideas, suggest a few manageable possibilities and see what she selects.

After the Interview

Immediately after the interview, make a few notes about what you learned. Summarize how this information will help you personalize recognition. Over the next few months, as you begin to recognize employees, track the frequency, purpose, and form of recognition given as well as the employees' reactions. By reviewing this information frequently, you can consider the following questions and respond accordingly:

Has an employee gone unrecognized for more than a month?

- Many managers say they have employees who aren't doing anything that merits recognition. In most cases, they aren't paying close enough attention to employee performance, or they're setting their expectations too high. Most employees are doing something worth recognizing. If you have an employee whose performance is so poor that there is really nothing to recognize, you need to take the appropriate steps to let the employee go.
- The problem may be the way the employee responded to past recognition. If an award was met with an embarrassed silence or the employee seemed disappointed with a new opportunity, it is time to ask more questions. Discover whether the recognition itself was inappropriate or whether some other factor is at work. Adjust your recognition as necessary to accommodate employee preferences.
- Often managers simply forget to recognize employee performance. It's difficult to establish a new habit. You can get busy and forget. Make the effort to get into the recognition habit, because appreciation makes work flow more smoothly and people more productive. Everything else becomes harder when you skip recognition. Skip recognition, and you will spend more time dealing with employee dissatisfaction and higher turnover. Invest the time in recognizing employees and watch your job get easier.

Remember the Gallup survey: people want recognition at least every seven days. As the manager, don't feel you have to offer all the recognition yourself. Recognition should be coming from a variety of sources. To increase the amount of recognition each employee receives, you can enlist the help of other people. Just don't abdicate all responsibility. Remember that recognition from you is typically the most highly regarded recognition that your employees receive.

Is most of the recognition employees are receiving taking one form?

- Variety requires creativity (or some good resource books) and a quick review of employee preferences. When you review preferences, you may recall that one employee would like to take a class, while another prefers lunch with you and a major client. Find ways to add variety while honoring employee preferences.

Recognition is an ongoing process. You need to follow up regularly with employees to see if your recognition efforts are on target. Talking about preferences will create the expectation of personalized recognition and lead to disappointment if you don't deliver. Continue to learn more about your employees. Do they enjoy skiing, golfing, or photography? Do they like public recognition? Are silly awards fun or stupid? Use what you learn to tailor recognition. Recognize employees frequently and in a variety of appropriate ways.

Interview Everyone

Having a conversation with every employee is time-consuming. It is also worth every minute spent doing it. Whether you do a formal interview or have casual hallway discussions over the course of several months, the insights you gain and the loyalty you build will more than justify the time it takes.

Managers Aren't the Only Ones Who Can Discover Preferences

It is important to reiterate that everyone can individualize recognition. The time you spend learning about the people you work with is, in itself, a significant form of recognition. Regardless of whether you are a manager or supervisor—or a team member, cubicle mate, or internal customer—when you learn a little something about the people around you, they feel more valued. Learn what they like to do in their spare time, what they like to eat, or what kind of music they enjoy. Your interest and concern will positively impact those relationships and allow you to recognize people more appropriately.

Putting It All Together

Once you know what people value, you can offer recognition that has specific meaning. You can recognize unique contributions with personalized rewards by doing two things.

First, when you give recognition, provide a complete description of the valued behavior or accomplishment, and tell how it helps the group or organization.

> Years ago I received a regional customer service award from a company that I represented. The regional manager presented the award to me at the annual regional meeting with all of my peers in attendance. I didn't know ahead of time that I had won. The manager began the presentation by reading the criteria for the award: consistent concern for customers, a high level of product knowledge, and a willingness to go the extra mile to ensure excellence in customer service. Then she read a lengthy client quote. At one point the quote became so specific I recognized the client and realized I was the winner. It was a very special moment. Fifteen years later the award still has significance for me. I knew what the company valued and knew someone had put a considerable amount of effort into verifying that I had met their standards. The detailed description of my contribution made the reward meaningful.

Second, offer recognition specifically selected for the recipient based on your knowledge of what that person values. In my case, I enjoyed the public praise, so the award was a good choice. I like to think my representative knew me well enough to know this of me. Had I disliked public attention, I wouldn't have the same fond memory of this award.

What about the employee's family? Should you be able to safely acknowledge them without worrying about whether your recognition is personalized? It seems reasonable. After all, it's your job to know the employee, not their family—isn't it? Consider what the wife of a top salesperson shared regarding the recognition she received:

> "My husband's company sent me a big gift basket when he became the top salesman. I really resented that he had to work many overtime hours with no days off in order to make top salesman. I was actively lobbying to get him to change jobs at the time."

The fruit basket reminded the wife of all the hours her husband had spent away from the family. It had an impact, but not the one his company wanted. The person arranging for the basket assumed the salesman's family supported his long hours. Had this person known this salesman a little better, management could have made a better choice. A certificate for dinner for the family, along with a note of understanding, would have had a more positive result.

Specific Contribution + Personalization = Meaningful Recognition

Consider a situation where someone adeptly facilitates the progress of a team meeting. You're a member of this team, though not necessarily the leader. You want to show your appreciation to the facilitator. If the facilitator appreciates public praise, the following might be an appropriate announcement:

> "This has been a productive meeting. Before we leave, I want to acknowledge Mai for keeping us focused on the meeting's key objective: naming our new product. At one

point we veered off into a discussion of product features. We made several other unintended 'detours,' and each time Mai brought us back to our objective tactfully but purposefully. Thank you, Mai."

For a private person, this kind of public attention would be uncomfortable. Offer her the same message, one-to-one after the meeting, or send an e-mail message, possibly copying her supervisor. Every person is different. One individual would like the opportunity to take a class. Another wants the chance to teach it. Make sure you know the preferences of the people you recognize.

Case Study—Recognition Misses the Mark

Use the following scenario to test your ability to recognize individual preferences:

April is in her mid-twenties, single, friendly, but a little shy. She is a willing worker who accepts new challenges. She loves her job as a journalist. To see her name on the byline of a hard news or human interest story makes her day. Much of her job satisfaction comes from her belief that she makes a difference in the community where she works. She is also proud of the reputation of "her" paper in the community.

As much as April loves her work, she also cherishes the time she has away from it. She has a close circle of friends who get together every Friday evening to cook a gourmet meal and talk about their week.

April's manager, Terrence, knows very little about April or what motivates her, but he does know that she will usually take on a challenge. A challenge is exactly what he has on his hands one Friday afternoon when the sportswriter goes home sick. Counting on April's willingness to pitch in, Terrence asks her to cover the football game at the local university that evening and have an article ready in the morning. April reluctantly agrees. She hurries her "real" news story and misses the Friday night dinner party. Saturday morning she turns in an excellent article.

At the Monday staff meeting, Terrence announces that they have a terrific new sportswriter on the team. He thinks he is offering positive recognition for April's accomplishment, but April is mortified. What went wrong? What could Terrence do differently?

Take a moment to go back through the story and notice what April values and what forms of recognition she might prefer. Note what you discover.

What Went Wrong?

Terrence senses April is a team player who values her ability to contribute to the overall quality of the paper. He knows that she is usually up to a challenge and uses that knowledge to get her to take on the sports assignment. He knows enough about her to get her to do the work—at least one time. To motivate April long-term, Terrence should take into account the following about April:

- Is shy and doesn't want praise in front of her coworkers
- Doesn't want to do sports stories
- Prefers hard news and human interest assignments
- Wants to make a difference in the community
- Has pride in the reputation of the paper in the community
- Values her time off to spend with friends
- Is interested in gourmet food
- Likes interesting challenges

April quickly discovers that Terrence is unaware of her interests and ambitions. She realizes he doesn't know what she values or, worse, doesn't care. Next time she'll be less willing to help out, and if it happens too many times, she will take her willingness to contribute elsewhere.

Getting It Right

Terrence could send April an e-mail, voice mail, or note recognizing her willingness to pitch in with quality work, even when the subject is one that doesn't interest her. That alone would go a long way with April. He could double the impact if he then rewarded her with any of the following:

- A choice assignment in either of her two areas of interest
- A gift certificate for her favorite restaurant or gourmet market
- A cooking lesson with a local chef

Like April, your people want personalized recognition. One-size-fits-all recognition gives them the impression that you care only about their achievements. If you don't take their preferences into account, they will assume you don't care about them as people.

Know what is important to your employees. Listen to what they have to say. Then recognize your people by giving them more of what they like and less of what they don't like. Give recognition that shows employees that they matter. Offer recognition that makes their day!

TAKING ACTION

- Learn more about the people around you. Find out what is important to them.
- Use what you learn to offer recognition that takes their interests and needs into account.

13

Dealing with the Fairness Paradox

A manager told me about a direct report who has been telecommuting very successfully. The employee is productive and conscientious and sees the opportunity to telecommute as something he has earned. It is an excellent form of recognition.

Now the manager wants to take away this opportunity because he is afraid other employees will see this situation as unfair. This manager knows that the more you single people out, the more likely you are to be perceived as unfair; and, like many managers and supervisors, he thinks that if he can't give everyone a certain form of recognition, he shouldn't give any to anyone. Faced with the fairness paradox, he has come up with a solution where everyone loses.

Treating Everyone the Same

Recognition, by its very nature, singles out individuals or groups of individuals.

Is it fair to single people out? Some employees would respond no, saying that everyone should be treated the same. If you have heard this comment from a few of the people in your group, you may also have noticed that the mediocre performers are often the ones who do the most complaining about fairness. So, what do you do? Let's start with what you *don't* do.

It is not fair to treat everyone the same!

If you think about the meaning of recognition, of really seeing and valuing the individual, you will realize that when you treat everyone identically, *no* recognition takes place.

A much better solution for the manager of the telecommuter in our example is to find different ways of recognizing the performance of other people on the team. I would be surprised if everyone even *wants* to telecommute. Chances are good that one person is more interested in fast-tracking career growth, while another would love to cross-train for a new position.

To be fair, you need to ensure that everyone has equal *opportunity* for recognition. When he was a director at Cisco Systems, Doug Purcell, now VP of Public Sector Service Sales, realized that his salespeople had more chances to receive recognition than did the support members of the team. He knew that sales support provided a critical role, without which salespeople would have difficulty succeeding. As part of his efforts to provide more balance, he implemented a quarterly award to be given to an outstanding individual whose work supports the efforts of the sales team. The award, a director's chair imprinted with the name of the award and the Cisco logo, was originally called the Director's Award and now is known as the Impact Award. According to Jeanne Martin, a recipient of the Director's Award, "It is always meaningful to be recognized in front of your peers, especially when your contributions are less obvious."

The Four Rules of Fairness

To be fair, we need to think in terms of equivalent recognition for equivalent performance.

Know individual preferences. This is the first step in providing equivalent recognition. If you've done your homework from the previous chapter, you know what the individuals on your team value. You should have a good understanding of the differences in their preferences. If so, you are ready for step 2.

> 1. Know individual preferences.
> 2. **Clarify the perceived value of recognition options.**
> 3. Align performance with the perceived value of the recognition.
> 4. Present your recognition message effectively.

Step 2 requires that you understand what is most valued within your organization. Whether your "organization" is an entire company or a project team, it is your job to understand what is most and least valued.

No two organizations are exactly the same, but in general perceived value fits the recognition hierarchy in the pyramid diagram on the next page. Significant dollar awards have the greatest perceived value, while a verbal thank-you has the least. Please note that this perceived value does not mean that a bonus is more *meaningful* than a thank-you. Perception of value has more to do with both the time and money you are willing to "spend" on each individual.

Recognition Fairness Hierarchy

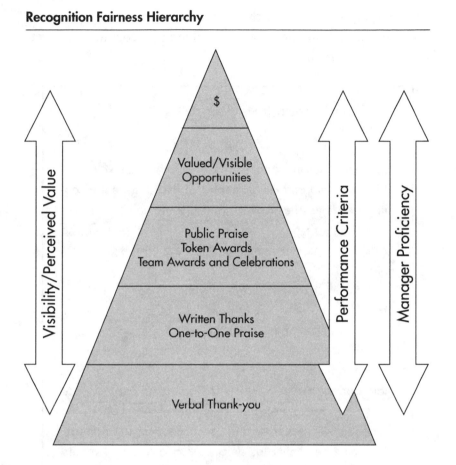

The higher you go on the pyramid, the more valued or visible the reward, and the riskier recognition gets. It becomes more likely that someone will say, "Unfair!" You might think that it would be safer to stay at the bottom levels of the hierarchy, except that many of the riskier options offer extremely meaningful recognition.

To be fair, you must clarify the perceived value of each recognition option. It is not an exact science, and you may have to adjust your pyramid as you go along. Get the help of your team to identify their recognition hierarchy.

The more public the recognition and the greater the perceived value, the more likely it is that your efforts will be seen as unfair.

The farther you move up the pyramid, the more important it becomes that you are proficient in delivering recognition and setting clear performance criteria.

The Recognition Hierarchy Pyramid

The recognition hierarchy pyramid helps clarify which recognition has the greatest risk of unfairness. Take a look at the pyramid and the examples of the forms that recognition can take. The arrow to the left shows that the greater the visibility or perceived value of the recognition, the greater the risk that someone will see that recognition as unfair.

As you scan the pyramid, you will see that public praise has a greater risk of perceived unfairness than private praise. The more visible the praise, the more chance there is that someone will believe it is unfair. Likewise, a written thank-you note can be displayed so it provides more opportunity for resentment than verbal appreciation.

In the example at the beginning of the chapter, the manager was concerned that the telecommuting opportunity would be viewed as unfair. As a visible and valued opportunity, he would be right—it does have the *potential* of being seen as unfair. But if the manager identifies a number of opportunities that occupy similar positions on the hierarchy, he can select different opportunities to recognize different individuals.

Opportunity is near the top of the recognition hierarchy. Money occupies the top position. Ironically, cash, gift cards, and gift certificates are the most risky and, at the same time, the least memorable of awards. Any monetary awards are equated with compensation; therefore, they are highly valued. Yet once the award is spent, the recognition is usually gone as well.

1. Know individual preferences.
2. Clarify the perceived value of recognition options.
3. **Align performance with the perceived value of the recognition.**
4. Present your recognition message effectively.

We have covered steps 1 and 2. Now let's look at step 3: align performance with the perceived value of the recognition we offer. If you look at the hierarchy again, you will see that the arrow to the immediate right of the pyramid is Performance Criteria. It is important to remember that the greater the value and visibility, the greater the need for solid criteria.

With step 3, the question you need to ask yourself is, in terms of performance, "What do I value?" Here is a list of common responses:

- Teamwork
- Customer service
- Innovation
- Entrepreneurial spirit

Let's say that we want to align the value of recognition to performance related to teamwork. To receive a verbal thank-you, team members need to demonstrate a single, small instance of teamwork. To receive a token award, the example of teamwork needs to be a bit more exceptional; and to receive valued and visible opportunities, the individual needs to consistently exemplify teamwork.

Develop a clear sense of what is significant and what is minor. In many cases, your list will be subjective. If you can make your criteria measurable, you increase the likelihood that your recognition will be perceived as fair. To learn how and what to measure, see Chapter 10.

1. Know individual preferences.
2. Clarify the perceived value of recognition options.
3. Align performance with the perceived value of the recognition.
4. **Present your recognition message effectively.**

The last arrow is Manager Proficiency. The more practiced you are in the art of recognition, the more likely you are to deliver recognition that is both fair and *perceived* as fair.

The first part of manager proficiency is your ability to communicate your criteria and effectively demonstrate that someone has met those criteria.

It takes practice to communicate a strong recognition message. Remember to keep your message accurate and specific. Start with verbal praise and appreciation. You will develop confidence in your ability to communicate what is most valued.

As your proficiency improves, you can safely select recognition options higher up the hierarchy. With proficiency, you can offer valuable and visible recognition, and everyone will have a clear understanding of why the recipient received this recognition.

Setting Expectations

The second part of manager proficiency is the ability to manage perception by managing expectations.

If you have followed the steps outlined here, you are offering fair recognition. To some extent, you have also managed the *perception* that recognition is fair—but not completely. Keep in mind that it is human nature to compare, and recognition is no exception. People will look at the recognition they receive and hold it up to the recognition that others are getting and think, "Am I getting my fair share?"

The hierarchy diagram shows that the types of recognition that receive the greatest scrutiny have the highest visibility and perceived value. The more public or desired the recognition, the more carefully you need to manage perception. Critical to managing perception is your ability to manage expectations. So, what expectations do you need to establish?

- **Performance will be awarded.** You need to communicate that the more impressive the performance, the more desirable the award. Performance criteria should be obvious to all. Don't keep your recognition criteria a secret. Of course, this means you have to be consistent in applying your criteria!
- **Comparison is futile.** Employees should know that fair does not mean identical. Make it clear that comparing is a waste of time. Set the expectation that each person will receive the rewards that are best suited to his or her preferences.

Fairness Assessment

Ask yourself:

- ☐ Am I setting realistic expectations?
- ☐ Am I aware of each individual's contribution?
- ☐ Am I rewarding team members based on performance and preference?

Fairness in Action

Your goal is to be fair. To achieve this goal, you need to differentiate based on performance. Top performers receive the most valued and visible recognition. Underperformers receive realistic assessment of their work with as much encouragement and praise as is appropriate.

You also have to consider preference when selecting equivalent recognition for equivalent performance. Here are two examples:

Praise: One person would love nothing more than to be pulled in front of the department and congratulated for an accomplishment. This doesn't mean you need to praise everyone who does something notable in the same public manner. Another person would prefer subtle praise: "John, you had an excellent idea for the new website. Would you mind describing it to the group?" These are equivalent forms of praise, both valued and visible.

Opportunity: A hardworking employee wants the chance to test her organizational skills. Reward her with the lead on a project. Another has school-age children and appreciates some flexibility in her schedule. Again, both are valued and visible while being quite different.

Both of these examples will be perceived as fair if you have set expectations that performance is rewarded and comparison futile.

Fairness is a matter of perception. If you have developed strong relationships with employees that are based on respect, employees will be inclined to see your recognition as fair.

TAKING ACTION

- Learn which forms of recognition are most valued within your culture. Don't be afraid to talk to your team about this topic. The more open the conversation, the greater the chance that the recognition that follows will be fair.
- Set clear performance criteria, particularly for the most valued and visible rewards.
- Have an ongoing conversation about rewards, performance, and expectations.

chapter 14

Recognition Is a Work in Progress

The Importance of Commitment and Planning

Recognition is never a quick fix. It requires time to create the kind of work environment where recognition is inherent and to build the kinds of relationships necessary to make recognition meaningful. Trust is established, relationships are built, and habits are solidified over the long term.

> According to Dave Densley, a small-business owner, "It's been about two years since I bought and read [*Make Their Day!*] and about a year now that I have been getting your e-mail tips. Guess what? It's only now that it is starting to sink in and I find myself implementing your advice in a more natural way. Isn't that crazy? One would think it would happen faster, but it hasn't for me."

Building a habit is critical to providing meaningful recognition. When managers begin to offer recognition, most employees take a wait-and-see approach. Most have seen, as Chris Hartsock of GMAC® says, "the flurry and fizzle" of a new recognition program. You will have to prove your commitment.

Although the need for commitment may seem obvious, the importance of planning isn't as clear. You may be effective with little or no planning. A bit of commitment and a lot of sincerity can go a long way. But if you want to offer consistent, fair, and frequent recognition, it helps to have a plan. Without one, recognition is likely to be sporadic and inconsistent.

Keeping One Ball in the Air

*Learning to offer effective recognition is
a little like learning to juggle.*

Start by trying to juggle four balls at once, and you're sure to drop them all.

When many managers begin to offer recognition, there is a tendency to start too big. Using a juggling analogy, they pick up too many balls at once.

Ball 1: They create a peer recognition program.
Ball 2: They commit to praising every person, every week.
Ball 3: They schedule a celebration for meeting a milestone.
Ball 4: They plan a friendly competition to improve service scores.

Overwhelmed, they find it's more difficult to stay committed and keep others committed to the process. It is likely that they will get discouraged and fail in their attempt to offer meaningful recognition. They drop *all* the balls.

*Whether you are learning to juggle or learning to
recognize effectively, it's better to start with one "ball"*

and learn proper form and timing before increasing
the number of balls you try to keep in the air.

Learning to juggle or recognize in such a methodical manner may not seem exciting, but you'll be more competent, and people will have more confidence in your capabilities if you do.

Pick up only one recognition ball to start:

☐ Write personalized anniversary cards noting accomplish-
ments for the year.
☐ Have regular one-on-one meetings with staff to discuss
whatever they wish.
☐ Begin to have weekly FASTER meetings.
☐ Celebrate a recent accomplishment.

Start Small, Evaluate, and Adjust

The basic steps to developing consistent, meaningful recognition are start small, evaluate, and adjust.

1. **Start small.** Choose whatever you like, just keep it manageable. Work on technique and form.
2. **Evaluate** what works well, uncover potential problems, and make sure resources are used effectively.
3. **Adjust.** Make necessary corrections; improve your timing and accuracy.

You might start by sending everyone a handwritten note outlining what each individual has done to support the team. Then, by gauging reactions and making adjustments, you can improve your ability to offer effective recognition. Then add another form of recognition or increase the frequency of what you did previously. By progressing slowly, you will keep recognition and expectations at a manageable level. You will have more success doing less than you would have if you set expectations too high and then failed to deliver.

Making a Plan

Making a recognition plan follows this three-step process:

Step 1: Determine the current state of recognition. Read the responses from any surveys your organization has completed, ask HR to administer a full assessment of your recognition proficiency, or talk with employees. It is difficult to know where to put your efforts without understanding employee perception. If you have a large team or are responsible for a major recognition effort, start with an employee survey and follow it up with focus groups or one-on-one interviews to really understand what is needed.

Step 2: Plan your recognition strategy. This might mean simply deciding how frequently you are going to personally thank each person. If you are taking on something more complex or sophisticated, lay out a complete plan to ensure that you can follow through and not disappoint your people.

Step 3: Commit to a long-term, graduated implementation. No matter what the size of your recognition effort, implementing recognition needs to be an ongoing cycle: implement, observe, evaluate the results, and then adapt and improve as you start the whole process again.

Let's take a closer look at each step.

Step 1: Determine the Current State of Recognition

Chefs taste the food as they prepare a meal. They don't add more seasoning without first sampling the flavor of the dish. If they did, they might end up adding too much salt or spice to a dish that is already salty or spicy enough. They taste the food because they want to know how existing flavors are working together. Tasting helps them figure out what is missing or how they can best complement what they already have.

The same principle works with employee recognition. Before you decide what would be complementary or what needs to change, you need to determine what you already have. You need to figure out what's working and what's not. To establish a starting point, assess your employees' satisfaction with existing recognition.

Use Job Satisfaction Surveys

As you've worked your way through this book, you will have discovered that many of the things that positively influence job satisfaction contain one or more of the elements of recognition. Because recognition and job satisfaction are so closely intertwined, measures of job satisfaction can be excellent gauges of the effectiveness of recognition.

If your organization isn't already surveying employees, you have some options.

- Encourage your management to conduct a survey. The information gathered will help with satisfaction, retention, and productivity. To do this they can purchase a standard job satisfaction survey or create their own. In the first edition, FedEx Freight West generously allowed reprinting of its Employee Quality of Worklife Survey.[1] To create consistency across FedEx, this survey is no longer in use, but it is still an excellent survey that you might want to emulate. It appears in the appendix.
- You might want to use the recognition survey also found in the appendix. Although it won't give as comprehensive a view of job satisfaction, it does provide a more in-depth look at recognition satisfaction. Use either survey with large departments, divisions, or the whole organization. For smaller groups, you are better off just talking to employees.

- Avoid making assumptions. Use the results of your survey as an opportunity to initiate discussions that will develop a clear picture of what employees want and need.
- Use the information you gather as the foundation for step 2.

Step 2: Plan Your Recognition Strategy

Do you have an idea of how you would like to recognize employees? If your idea is more complex than instituting a weekly lunchtime get-together to celebrate successes, you need a plan!

Imagine you're the manager of a department of thirty people. You do a survey and discover that only 25 percent of your employees believe they get appropriate recognition. Further probing uncovers dissatisfaction with two company-sponsored programs. It seems no one is very happy with the monogrammed notepads the company gives out after ten years of dedicated service, and most people think $5 gift cards are an inappropriate way to acknowledge people whose suggestions lead to major cost-saving improvements.

Further discussion reveals that employees would like to choose their own rewards. As the manager, you know that you can opt out of these two company-sponsored programs if you choose. You can use your portion of the very meager recognition budget as you see fit. You wonder if it's possible to make better use of the limited funds available.

You begin to assess the rest of your resources. Talking to employees, you discover that your whole department is eager to get involved in the recognition process. You ask for volunteers for a recognition planning team and set a goal to repeat the survey in four months to see if the team can achieve 75 percent satisfaction.

The first thing the team does is to confirm your decision to scrap the notepads and certificates. They decide, with the current budget limitations, meaningful individual rewards aren't possible. The team thinks it would be more fun to use the money for an auction. You ask how an auction will provide recognition. The team leader explains that the auction will be based around a peer recognition program. The team plans to print "Thanks for . . ." cards. Everyone in the department will receive a supply of the cards to use to recognize their coworkers. The cards will have space for the giver to describe why they are saying thanks. The cards will also have a tear-off stub for recipients to use as a token for bidding in the quarterly auction.

The team plans to use the entire recognition budget for printing and auction items, so they decide to ask each employee to bring a favorite food to share on the day of the auction. This way they can add to the fun with a celebratory lunch. You offer to act as master of ceremonies for the event and plan to use the opportunity to express your own words of appreciation.

Identify Resources

Before you decide what you are going to do, you need to know what resources you have to work with. As the last example shows, your resources will include both your budget and the people who can assist you. You don't need a lot of money. You can even provide great recognition with no money at all. Still, you will be more effective if you know what you have to work with and plan for how it will be used.

In the previous example, your team knew their budget and carefully planned for its use. Chances of success are very good! Now consider an example where the manager doesn't plan ahead.

Your manager begins her own recognition program. The first time she recognizes you, it is for getting your status reports from the last twelve months in on time and error-free. As a reward, you receive an overnight trip for two to the city. You think, "Wow, this is great!" Your manager provides a number of people in your department with similar rewards. She also offers her sincere appreciation for a job well done.

The next time she recognizes you, it is for mentoring another supervisor. Along with your manager's praise, you receive two movie passes. You are confused; you were sure your manager valued the mentoring you provided more than your timely, error-free status reports. So you wonder, "Am I inadequate as a mentor? Is mentoring really as important as I thought?" Throughout the rest of the year, you continue to receive your share of praise and thank-yous, but no additional rewards, even though you do some remarkable work. You continue to have doubts about what your manager values and the quality of your work.

In this example, you didn't know your manager depleted her recognition budget early in the year. Although she continued to offer you quality recognition, the accompanying rewards were inconsistent. That inconsistency led to confusion. The rewards that were supposed to reinforce recognition only served to muddy it.

Without some sense of what you can spend, there is a tendency to use up a large portion of available funds early on and then fall back on free recognition. Employee expectations are set in the early stages, so when rewards diminish over time, it creates confusion and disappointment. You want to use the highest-value awards to recognize the highest-value accomplishments, and you want to present some awards later in the year in order to maintain excitement. The only way you can do this is with planning.

What if you have no budget for recognition and aren't likely to get one? In most cases, you can still find money for recognition. Often, with a little creativity, you can make the line items on your budget serve double-duty.

A large professional association with no budget for recognition has budgeted for a monthly member newsletter. The director decides to add a regular feature to this newsletter. It will highlight a different employee each month, describing the employee's job function, interests, and contribution to the association. Members will benefit from the addition because they will learn more about the people who work on their behalf. Employees will benefit from much-needed recognition.

When you look for money for recognition, look for funds that can serve two purposes. Some sources to consider include funds set aside for bonuses, employee events or celebrations, training, or the manager's discretionary use. These funds can provide additional opportunities for recognition. Make them serve both their intended purpose and your recognition strategy.

Set Realistic Goals and Time Frames

In the spirit of not overcommitting, consider what it will take to implement your plan. You want realistic goals and deadlines.

In the auction example, you set a goal to repeat the survey in four months and show an improvement from 25 percent to 75 percent. Can you achieve this goal? Possibly, but it probably isn't very realistic to expect that kind of improvement from one peer recognition program. A better goal would be 50 percent.

Is the four-month deadline realistic? To see if it is, identify smaller goals or phases, and estimate the time it will take to complete each. Your team decides the following are the critical phases, and estimates the time each will take.

Phase 1: Design and print the cards—four weeks.
Phase 2: Develop and communicate criteria—three weeks.
Phase 3: Run the card program—three months.

Phase 4: Select auction items—two weeks.

Phase 5: Plan a celebration—one week.

Phase 6: Hold the auction and celebration—two hours.

If you total the time required, it would add up to approximately six months. But this doesn't take into account that many of these phases can happen concurrently. The people on your team can complete the first two phases at the same time, so the card program can begin in four weeks. Phases 4 and 5 can both take place while the card program is running. You will be ready to hold the auction and resurvey your department in four months—right on schedule.

Step 3: Commit to a Continually Evolving Implementation

Remember the juggling balls. Recognition works best when you start small, gain competence and confidence, and then slowly expand your efforts. Employees respond favorably when they see that recognition isn't a flavor-of-the-week initiative. Step 3 creates a cycle of continuous improvement that makes recognition most effective: implement, observe, evaluate, and improve.

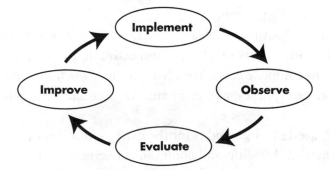

Implement

With your plan in place, you are ready to begin the implementation. Complete the steps as you have planned them. As you implement, don't forget to communicate your recognition plan to those who are involved. Communicating your plan isn't as important with informal recognition, but if you are planning a formal program, it becomes critical. It is very important that you provide adequate information about what your employees can expect from your program. Describe the kind of recognition you'll be offering and what you're looking for in terms of behavior and accomplishment. If your surveys and questionnaires uncovered recognition problems, acknowledge these and describe how you plan to remedy them. Invite employees to offer feedback as the implementation proceeds. To improve the odds of long-term success, encourage open communication throughout the process.

Observe and Evaluate

Observe what works and what doesn't. Evaluate the results of your efforts. The question to ask is "Are we having the impact that we want to have?" If the answer is no, you need to know why.

> A vice president told me that while he showed appreciation and recognized his employees, no one ever reciprocated. He said employees were quick to bring him their complaints when he didn't deliver, but they never acknowledged any improvement in *his* performance. In a later conversation I had with one of his managers, we discussed the importance of "recognizing up." The manager told me his VP didn't like compliments. He said he had attempted to acknowledge his VP during a meeting and observed that the VP was clearly uncomfortable. I asked him to consider that it might not be

the compliment but something else that had made the VP uncomfortable. He decided to try a different forum for offering appreciation. After our conversation, he sent the VP an e-mail thanking him for his help on a recent project and received back a very positive response.

Observe how people respond to the recognition you give. Use follow-up discussions and surveys to gain more information. Look at people's reactions to recognition, but also consider other factors. Have attitudes changed? Are people more productive and self-directed? In evaluating your success, also consider the changes recognition may have had on your operations. The same measures you used to track achievement will help you evaluate the impact of recognition on your operations. With measures in place, you will be able to determine whether costs, safety violations, or the number of sick days taken have decreased. You will be able to show whether outcomes such as productivity, percentage of repeat business, or the close rate on leads have increased.

Compare where you were before to where you are now. The information you gather will help you figure out what is working and what can be improved. It will help give your recognition greater impact.

Improve

Now that you have analyzed and clarified your results, you can identify your strengths and weaknesses. Congratulate yourself on what you have accomplished so far. Build on your strengths. Figure out what you can do to improve.

After completing the auction project mentioned earlier, you survey your department to find you have 45 percent employee satisfaction. That is an improvement of 20 percent—

good progress—but still far from being an excellent rating. You look for ways to improve it. Further discussions with employees reveal that while they like the peer recognition program, they want more recognition directly from you, the manager.

As you begin the cycle of improvement, you set a new goal: 65 percent satisfaction at the end of the next three months.

Your plan:

- Continue the "Thanks for . . ." peer card program as implemented.
- Use the "Thanks for . . ." card program for your own on-the-spot recognition.
- Have a contribution conversation (see Chapter 12) with your two supervisors and five team leads, completing and acting on all seven conversations within two months.

To complete this cycle, you implement your plan, observe and evaluate the results, make the necessary changes to improve, and prepare for the next cycle.

Where Do You Go from Here?

Employees crave meaningful recognition. When they talk about the recognition they receive, they're talking about how valued they feel. To help the people you work with feel valued, you need to focus on the essence of what recognition is. Instead of offering recognition at a superficial level, you need to remember to look at recognition in the bigger context and over the long term. Recognition isn't a plaque; it's the meaning behind the plaque. It's about building relationships and taking a personal, genuine interest in people and their preferences. So long as you do that and continue to look for ways to refine the recognition that you offer, employees will feel recognized. That collective feeling, in turn, will boost morale, productivity, and profitability—and everybody wins.

TAKING ACTION

- Commit to a long-term solution to your employees' recognition needs.
- For help building a recognition habit, sign up for weekly recognition tips at www.maketheirday.com.
- Take on only as much as you can accomplish successfully.
- Ask questions. Learn what is working and what isn't.
- Plan carefully and act consistently.
- Reap the rewards of recognition that works.

Recognition Survey

Circle the answer that best describes your feelings

1. I feel appreciated for a job well done.

| STRONGLY AGREE | AGREE | NEITHER AGREE NOR DISAGREE | DISAGREE | STRONGLY DISAGREE |

2. My opinions matter to the people I work with.

| STRONGLY AGREE | AGREE | NEITHER AGREE NOR DISAGREE | DISAGREE | STRONGLY DISAGREE |

3. My supervisor respects my judgment.

| STRONGLY AGREE | AGREE | NEITHER AGREE NOR DISAGREE | DISAGREE | STRONGLY DISAGREE |

4. My supervisor recognizes me for my hard work.

| STRONGLY AGREE | AGREE | NEITHER AGREE NOR DISAGREE | DISAGREE | STRONGLY DISAGREE |

5. I know what our organization values.

| STRONGLY AGREE | AGREE | NEITHER AGREE NOR DISAGREE | DISAGREE | STRONGLY DISAGREE |

6. My work contributes to our goals and strategies.

| STRONGLY AGREE | AGREE | NEITHER AGREE NOR DISAGREE | DISAGREE | STRONGLY DISAGREE |

7. My contributions are recognized in a way that reinforces the goals and strategies of the organization.

| STRONGLY AGREE | AGREE | NEITHER AGREE NOR DISAGREE | DISAGREE | STRONGLY DISAGREE |

8. I know what is expected from me.

| STRONGLY AGREE | AGREE | NEITHER AGREE NOR DISAGREE | DISAGREE | STRONGLY DISAGREE |

9. My supervisor works with me to develop my individual goals.

| STRONGLY AGREE | AGREE | NEITHER AGREE NOR DISAGREE | DISAGREE | STRONGLY DISAGREE |

10. Recognition reinforces my individual work goals.

| STRONGLY AGREE | AGREE | NEITHER AGREE NOR DISAGREE | DISAGREE | STRONGLY DISAGREE |

Recognition Survey, Continued

11. My supervisor knows and cares about what is important to me.

STRONGLY AGREE	AGREE	NEITHER AGREE NOR DISAGREE	DISAGREE	STRONGLY DISAGREE

12. Quality is valued within my work group.

STRONGLY AGREE	AGREE	NEITHER AGREE NOR DISAGREE	DISAGREE	STRONGLY DISAGREE

13. I receive some sort of praise or recognition every week.

STRONGLY AGREE	AGREE	NEITHER AGREE NOR DISAGREE	DISAGREE	STRONGLY DISAGREE

14. My coworkers appreciate my contribution.

STRONGLY AGREE	AGREE	NEITHER AGREE NOR DISAGREE	DISAGREE	STRONGLY DISAGREE

15. The company recognizes both teams and individuals for their contributions.

STRONGLY AGREE	AGREE	NEITHER AGREE NOR DISAGREE	DISAGREE	STRONGLY DISAGREE

16. I receive appropriate opportunities for growth and development.

STRONGLY AGREE	AGREE	NEITHER AGREE NOR DISAGREE	DISAGREE	STRONGLY DISAGREE

17. We have regular opportunities for fun at work.

STRONGLY AGREE	AGREE	NEITHER AGREE NOR DISAGREE	DISAGREE	STRONGLY DISAGREE

18. I know how to offer recognition to my coworkers.

STRONGLY AGREE	AGREE	NEITHER AGREE NOR DISAGREE	DISAGREE	STRONGLY DISAGREE

19. My coworkers know how to acknowledge my contributions.

STRONGLY AGREE	AGREE	NEITHER AGREE NOR DISAGREE	DISAGREE	STRONGLY DISAGREE

20. The recognition I receive is appropriate for me.

STRONGLY AGREE	AGREE	NEITHER AGREE NOR DISAGREE	DISAGREE	STRONGLY DISAGREE

21. The most deserving groups and individuals are usually recognized for their contributions.

STRONGLY AGREE	AGREE	NEITHER AGREE NOR DISAGREE	DISAGREE	STRONGLY DISAGREE

22. My supervisor knows and respects me.

STRONGLY AGREE	AGREE	NEITHER AGREE NOR DISAGREE	DISAGREE	STRONGLY DISAGREE

23. Awards and incentives reinforce high performance.

STRONGLY AGREE	AGREE	NEITHER AGREE NOR DISAGREE	DISAGREE	STRONGLY DISAGREE

24. My supervisor sets a good example for how we should acknowledge each other.

STRONGLY AGREE	AGREE	NEITHER AGREE NOR DISAGREE	DISAGREE	STRONGLY DISAGREE

Notice that some of the statements on the recognition survey look at recognition in terms of general appreciation, appreciation from a supervisor or manager, or appreciation among coworkers. Other statements look at recognition as a natural outcome of quality work. Others consider whether recognition is fair and frequent, or whether appropriate behavior is being modeled.

If you have existing recognition programs, be sure to assess those as well. Add your own statements to the survey. You might use statements such as "The peer-nominated Customer Service Champion Award usually identifies the most deserving recipient," or "Employee Appreciation Day is a worthwhile recognition opportunity." The responses you receive will provide a good indication of the effectiveness of your programs.

FedEx Freight Employee Quality of Worklife Survey

FedEx Freight has generously allowed me to reprint their Quality of Worklife Survey for your use. When this survey first appeared in *Make Their Day* it was the primary survey tool of FedEx Freight. For organizational consistency, it has now been replaced by the Gallup Q12. The Quality of Worklife Survey remains a good example of a general job satisfaction survey. It addresses key areas of workplace satisfaction including compensation, expectations, policies, work environment, relationships, fairness, and pride of work. You are free to reproduce all or part of this survey within your organization.

FedEx Freight used job, location, and department categories to help identify where job satisfaction excelled and where it lagged behind.

Service Center/Maintenance/Field Sales

Place a ☑ in the appropriate job classification box
and another ☑ in the appropriate location box

❏ Maintenance ❏ Hostler/Fueler ❏ Dockworker
❏ Field Salesperson ❏ Linehaul Driver ❏ Ops
❏ Field Sales Clerical ❏ Local/P&D Driver ❏ Ops Supervisor

❏ Alaska ❏ Las Vegas
❏ Albuquerque ❏ Phoenix
❏ Bend ❏ Pocatello
❏ Boise ❏ Portland
❏ Chico ❏ Reno
❏ Colorado Springs ❏ Sacramento
❏ Denver ❏ Salem
❏ El Paso ❏ Salt Lake City
❏ Eugene ❏ San Diego
❏ Eureka ❏ San Fernando Valley
❏ Flagstaff ❏ San Luis Obispo
❏ Gardena ❏ Seattle
❏ Hawaii ❏ Tacoma
❏ Huntington Park ❏ Tucson
❏ Kingman ❏ Twin Falls

General Office/Administrative Departments/CAS

Place a ☑ in the appropriate department box

- ❑ Accounting
- ❑ Credit & Collections & Invoicing
- ❑ Cash Application, Error Controls
- ❑ Central Line Control
- ❑ Claims
- ❑ Claims Prevention
- ❑ OPS Planning & Engineering
- ❑ Customer Service
- ❑ Customer Mgmt & Switchboard – San Jose
- ❑ Customer Billing Assurance
- ❑ Human Resources
- ❑ Info Technology
- ❑ Inside Sales
- ❑ Market Analysis
- ❑ Corporate Communications
- ❑ Product Marketing
- ❑ Corporate Account Sales

Breakdown by category can be extremely valuable because it can pinpoint trouble spots within your organization. A poor score in a single location tells you that you need to learn more about what is causing the dissatisfaction in that location. Breakdown by category can also create challenges in maintaining the anonymity of survey respondents. For example, if you have one sales representative at a satellite office, a breakdown by job and location may cause this sales representative to be less than candid.

FedEx Freight Employee Quality of Worklife Survey, Continued

Circle the answer that best describes your feelings

	STRONGLY AGREE	AGREE	NEITHER AGREE NOR DISAGREE	DISAGREE	STRONGLY DISAGREE
1. When I arrive at work, I feel welcome.	YES	yes	neither	no	NO
2. I enjoy my job and the work I do.	YES	yes	neither	no	NO
3. I have a clear understanding of what's expected of me at work.	YES	yes	neither	no	NO
4. I feel a sense of control over my day-to-day work activities.	YES	yes	neither	no	NO
5. I feel appreciated for a job well done.	YES	yes	neither	no	NO
6. I am respected and I feel like part of a family.	YES	yes	neither	no	NO
7. I am proud to be part of FedEx Freight.	YES	yes	neither	no	NO
8. I am paid fairly compared with other FedEx Freight employees.	YES	yes	neither	no	NO
9. My total compensation compares favorably to similar jobs at other companies.	YES	yes	neither	no	NO
10. My supervisor is interested in my suggestions and ideas.	YES	yes	neither	no	NO
11. I have many opportunities to express my concerns to my supervisor.	YES	yes	neither	no	NO

FedEx Freight Employee Quality of Worklife Survey, Continued

Circle the answer that best describes your feelings	STRONGLY AGREE	AGREE	NEITHER AGREE NOR DISAGREE	DISAGREE	STRONGLY DISAGREE
12. My supervisor recognizes and rewards hard work and extra effort.	YES	yes	neither	no	NO
13. My supervisor keeps me informed about matters that affect me.	YES	yes	neither	no	NO
14. My supervisor supports me in my efforts to work safely.	YES	yes	neither	no	NO
15. My supervisor is approachable, easy to talk with.	YES	yes	neither	no	NO
16. My supervisor listens to my concerns and responds quickly.	YES	yes	neither	no	NO
17. FedEx Freight's work rules and policies are fair.	YES	yes	neither	no	NO
18. FedEx Freight's safety programs are effective.	YES	yes	neither	no	NO
19. FedEx Freight provides good benefits, health insurance, vacations, etc.	YES	yes	neither	no	NO
20. The President and Vice Presidents are interested in my suggestions and ideas.	YES	yes	neither	no	NO
21. The President and Vice Presidents are approachable, easy to talk with.	YES	yes	neither	no	NO
22. FedEx Freight is a better place to work than other trucking companies.	YES	yes	neither	no	NO
23. During the past year, I have recommended FedEx Freight as a place to work.	YES	yes	neither	no	NO
24. I have thought about leaving FedEx Freight because of unfair treatment on the job.	YES	yes	neither	no	NO

How can FedEx Freight improve as a place to work or as an industry leader? (include additional sheets if needed)

Books

The following are just a few of the books that will help you create the kind of work environment where employees feel recognized. Some focus on inherent recognition, some provide fun ideas that will spur your creativity, and others teach the specifics of goal setting and measurement—important elements of recognition.

For Managers

Building a Habit

Ventrice, Cindy. *Recognition Strategies That Work*. Santa Cruz, CA: Potential Unlimited Publishing, 2007. The companion guide to *Make Their Day!* that helps build strong recognition skills and habits.

Leadership Principles

Buckingham, Marcus, and Curt Coffman. *First, Break All the Rules: What the World's Greatest Managers Do Differently*. New York: Simon & Schuster, 1999. A classic book that introduces several key concepts: identifying what peak performers want, playing to employee strengths, and focusing on top performers.

Goldsmith, Marshall. *What Got You Here Won't Get You There*. New York: Hyperion, 2007. An outstanding book that reveals 20 Bad Habits of Ineffective Leaders.

Kaye, Beverly L., and Sharon Jordan-Evans. *Love 'Em or Lose 'Em: Getting Good People to Stay*. San Francisco: Berrett-Koehler, 2008. Retaining your best people is always a critical issue. This revised edition of the classic book offers practical A–Z management advice.

Rath, Tom, and Donald O. Clifton. *How Full Is Your Bucket?* New York: Gallup Press, 2004. A quick read that introduces Gallup research on the frequency of praise.

Sanders, Tim. *The Likeability Factor*. New York: Three Rivers Press, 2006. This book is designed to help you build self-awareness in how you connect with others.

Watkins, Michael. *The First 90 Days*. Boston: Harvard Business School Press, 2003. A book that will show you how to get off to a good start with a new team.

Recognition Ideas

Hemsath, Dave. *301 More Ways to Have Fun at Work*. San Francisco: Berrett-Koehler, 2001.

Hemsath, Dave, and Leslie Yerkes. *301 Ways to Have Fun at Work*. San Francisco: Berrett-Koehler, 1997.

Nelson, Bob. *1001 Ways to Reward Employees*. New York: Workman Publishing, 2005. A classic best-seller for recognition ideas.

For Training Developers

Ventrice, Cindy. *Recognition Strategies That Work*. Santa Cruz, CA: Potential Unlimited Publishing, 2007. The companion guide to *Make Their Day!* that helps build strong recognition skills and habits. Contains many activities and exercises suitable for training programs. The fifteen-week study guide provides reinforcement of the *Make Their Day!* philosophy.

For Recognition Program Developers

Gladwell, Malcolm. *Tipping Point*. New York: Little, Brown, 2002. Important information about developing program momentum, as well as the people who communicate your message and determine the success of your program.

Heath, Chip, and Dan Heath. *Made to Stick*. New York: Random House, 2007. You want the message of your program to "stick." This book will explain how to get attention and keep it.

Nelson, Bob, and Dean Spitzer. *1001 Rewards & Recognition Fieldbook*. New York: Workman Publishing, 2002. An excellent resource for any program developer.

Niven, Paul R. *Balanced Scorecard Step-by-Step: Maximizing Performance and Maintaining Results*. New York: Wiley, 2002. Helpful in the process of setting criteria.

Rath, Tom. *Vital Friends*. New York: Gallup Press, 2006. An in-depth look at relationships at work. Its concepts will help you create more effective peer recognition programs.

Smith, Douglas K. *Make Success Measurable! A Mindbook-Workbook for Setting Goals and Taking Action*. New York: Wiley, 1999. Will help with goal and metric development.

Ventrice, Cindy. *The Secret to Recognition Programs That Work*. Santa Cruz, CA: Potential Unlimited Publishing, 2008. Provides crucial considerations for anyone developing a recognition program.

Websites

www.maketheirday.com On this site you will find a current
resource listing as well as the latest recognition-related
information. You can sign up for a free weekly recognition tip and find information about the author's speaking
engagements and workshops.

www.recognition.org The website for Recognition Professionals
International. The organization provides a forum for
information and best practices around recognition.

acknowledgments

I am grateful for the encouragement and support of the entire Berrett-Koehler team who helped *Make Their Day!* become a best-selling book on recognition and made this second edition possible.

As with the first edition, I am indebted to my generous friends, clients, colleagues, and readers who have provided their support and insights and who, in many cases, allowed me to tell their stories. I appreciate each and every one of you.

I also want to thank my contacts at the organizations mentioned throughout the book. These people have shared best practices and lessons learned, as well as their tips for success.

Many people helped me update the original stories or determine that the essence of the story as told in the first edition was timeless and required no change. Their organizations are Wells Fargo Bank, Griffin Hospital, The Container Store, Microsoft Business Solutions, Graniterock, Design Octaves, FedEx Freight, University of California–Santa Cruz, LSI Logic, Xilinx, Plante & Moran, Raytek, Remedy and Pella Windows & Doors.

My gratitude also to those who helped bring fresh examples from Google, Best Buy, the British Columbia Ministry of Environment, the Graduate Management Admissions Council (GMAC®), the British Columbia Lottery Corporation, Home Hardware, Wells Fargo, and Cisco Systems.

Finally, my thanks to my husband Gary, because without his help and support, none of my work would be possible.

notes

Preface

1. It's difficult to differentiate money spent on recognition from that spent on incentives. Harold Stolovich, Richard Clark, and Steven Condly, authors of "Incentive, Motivation and Workplace Performance: Research and Best Practices" (available through the Professional Society for Performance Improvement), estimate $117 billion is spent on incentives, including variable pay. My far more conservative $18 billion estimate for both incentives (excluding variable pay) and recognition is based on the following data: In 2002, the National Association of Employee Recognition (now Recognition Professionals International) estimated $2 billion was spent on trophies, plaques, and other engravable awards. "The Incentive Merchandise and Travel Marketplace 2000" study estimated $12 billion is spent each year on travel, merchandise, and gift certificates. No figures were available on cash awards, such as spot bonuses and team awards, so I estimated a very conservative $4 billion.
2. From "ISPI 2002 Incentives Motivation and Workplace Performance."
3. WorldatWork reported in 2008 that 89 percent of respondents had a recognition program in place.
4. Tom Rath and Donald O. Clifton reported Gallup's findings in their book *How Full Is Your Bucket?* (New York: Gallup, 2004).

Introduction

1. Revenue overstatement and resignations were reported by United Press International, May 6, 2002.

2. Peregrine Systems being notified of NASDAQ's intent to delist was reported by the Associated Press, June 27, 2002.
3. Bob Tagg, Director of Customer Support Americas at Remedy, reported Remedy statistics on layoffs and customer satisfaction and revenue.

Chapter 2

1. There is an ongoing debate whether external motivators or incentives work. Alfie Kohn has written many books and articles on the topic, including *Punished by Rewards* (Boston: Houghton Mifflin, 1999) and an article for the *Harvard Business Review*, "Why Incentive Plans Cannot Work." In contrast, Harold Stolovitch, Richard Clark, and Steven Condly did a meta-analysis of all the research on the topic. They found that incentives positively and strongly influence performance. Their findings, "Incentive, Motivation and Workplace Performance: Research and Best Practices," are available through the Professional Society for Performance Improvement.
2. See David C. McClelland, *The Achievement Motive* (New York: Appleton-Century-Crofts, 1953); *Power: The Inner Experience* (New York: Irvington, 1975).
3. In *The Motivation to Work* (New York: Wiley, 1959), Fredrick Herzberg established his hygiene theory that stated that certain factors such as working conditions, salary, and benefits aren't motivators, but the lack of these factors leads to employee dissatisfaction.

Chapter 3

1. Steven Covey talks about the emotional bank account in his book *The Seven Habits of Highly Effective People* (New York: Simon & Schuster, 1990).
2. The name of the award was changed to allow for the director's anonymity.

Chapter 4

1. The Make Their Day Most Meaningful Recognition Survey 2007 analyzed meaningful recognition for cost, whom it came from,

whether it was team or individual recognition, and who was present at the time the recognition was given.

2. The survey from Maritz Research of Fenton, Missouri, included one thousand employees.
3. The Make Their Day Preference Survey 2008 of 845 employees, primarily from North America, looked at preferences in awards, frequency, work environment, and relationship with managers.

Chapter 9

1. Marcus Buckingham and Curt Coffman, *First, Break All the Rules: What the World's Greatest Managers Do Differently* (New York: Simon & Schuster, 1999).

Chapter 10

1. *The Toastmaster* reported in its October 2000 issue that the Grand Pioneer club in Amherst, New York, had developed the Terrific Toastmaster Award as a way to encourage leadership among its members.

Chapter 11

1. The Make Their Day Preference Survey 2008 of 845 employees, primarily from North America, looked at recognition preferences across generations and years in the workforce.
2. The What's Working Study by Mercer, 2008.

Chapter 12

1. See Peter F. Drucker, *Management Challenges for the 21st Century* (New York: HarperBusiness, 1999).

Chapter 14

1. The Quality of Worklife Survey is provided with the permission of Tom Suchevits, Vice President of Human Resources, FedEx Freight West.

index

Cindy Ventrice is an advocate of manager-driven recognition and has helped hundreds of companies successfully embrace this approach within their organizations.

She began her career working with technology solutions for small business. In that capacity, she helped hundreds of organizations computerize their systems, acting as adviser, project manager, technical resource, and trainer. She had the opportunity to work on many diverse projects in a wide range of industries, including technology, nonprofit, government, health care, manufacturing, trade, service, education, and tourism, and in the process developed a comprehensive understanding of business operations.

As a recognition advocate, she has worked with managers and supervisors from around the world in both the public and private sectors, teaching them how to improve loyalty and productivity with recognition. Her clients have included Cisco Systems, MIT, Bell Canada, Wells Fargo, and State Farm Insurance.

A frequent keynote speaker and active member of the National Speakers Association, Cindy addresses audiences on issues ranging from motivating volunteers to retaining the best employees and keeping them happy and productive. A longtime member of the improvisational theater community, she brings what she has learned as an improviser to her programs, injecting fun and interactivity into every keynote and training session.

Cindy is continually improving her knowledge of employee recognition. In the past two years she has completed two recognition studies: one on what makes recognition meaningful and the other on generational preferences.

She has been quoted for her expertise by media as diverse as the *New York Times* and the *Costco Connection* and has been interviewed on major radio stations nationwide on "How to Give Your Rotten Boss a Makeover."

Cindy grew up in the San Francisco Bay Area and later graduated with a BA from the education department of San Jose State University. She now lives in Santa Cruz, California, with her husband, Gary. Cindy uses the recognition techniques presented in *Make Their Day!* in nearly every aspect of her life, from marriage to work relationships and even her relationship with her mechanic!

For information about services and programs, you can contact:

CINDY VENTRICE
Potential Unlimited
PO Box 3437
Santa Cruz, CA 95063
Phone: (831) 476-4224
E-mail: cventrice@maketheirday.com
Web site: www.maketheirday.com